Einstein

Einstein

P D Smith

HAUS PUBLISHING · LONDON

For Avril and Bernard

First published in Great Britain in 2003 by
Haus Publishing Limited
32 Store Street
London WC1E 7BS

Copyright © P D Smith, 2003

The moral right of the authors has been asserted

A CIP catalogue record for this book
is available from the British Library

ISBN 1-904341-15-2 (paperback)
ISBN 1-904341-14-4 (hardback)

Designed and typeset in Albertina at Libanus Press, Marlborough

Printed and bound by Graphicom in Vicenza, Italy

Front cover: photograph of Albert Einstein courtesy of AKG London
Back cover: caricature of Einstein by David Levine

Contents

Concern for the man himself and his fate must always form the chief interest of all technical endeavours. Never forget this in the midst of your diagrams and equations.

ALBERT EINSTEIN [1]

Maths, Music, and Magnetism
1879 – 1894

Albert Einstein was born in the south German city of Ulm on 14 March 1879 at 11.30 on a bright but chilly spring morning. He could not have chosen a more suitable city. For one thing its motto is *Ulmense sunt mathematici*: the people of Ulm are mathematicians. The spire of Ulm's cathedral rises higher than any other, towering over the River Danube on its long eastbound journey out of Swabia, a region whose schools produced the philosopher G W F Hegel (1770–1831) and the poet Friedrich Hölderlin (1770–1843). The novelist Hermann Hesse (1877–1962), who was born in the Swabian Black Forest community of Calw just two years earlier than Einstein, described Ulm as an 'extremely beautiful and unusual city'.[2] Ulm is now part of Baden-Württemberg, a state that counts among its sons the 15th-century astrologer and alchemist Johannes Faust. In Goethe's great play, Faust came to personify mankind's ceaseless quest to understand and control nature, a quest Einstein was to make his own.

Einstein thought that a person's place of birth was as important *as one's origin from one's mother.* He wrote: *I therefore think of Ulm with gratitude, because it combines artistic tradition with a simple and sound*

Hesse, who like Einstein later emigrated to Switzerland, visited Ulm in 1926: 'I had not forgotten the city wall or the Metzgerturm, or the cathedral choir or the townhall, these images superimposed upon the images of memory differed little from them; on the other hand there were innumerable new scenes which I saw as though for the first time, age-old fishermen's houses standing askew in the dark water, little gnomes' houses on the city wall, proud burghers' houses in the narrow streets, here an odd gable, there a noble portal.'[3]

character.[4] As well as inheriting these qualities, Einstein never lost his Swabian accent, or his taste for the region's cooking, a taste shared with his second wife, who was also born in Swabia. Einstein's birth certificate states that his family lived at 135 Bahnhofstrasse, a street that runs from the main station to the cathedral. In 1944 their four-storey apartment building was destroyed by allied bombing, along with much of the historic city centre. But in spite of Ulm's motto, Einstein never claimed to be a mathematician. The physicist who wrote the most famous scientific equation, $E=mc^2$, once reassured a student, telling her: *Don't worry about your difficulties in mathematics; I can assure you that mine are still greater.*[5]

Einstein was born in the same year as the novelist E M Forster (1879–1970) and the Swiss painter Paul Klee (1879–1940), who grew up near Bern, the city where Einstein would work on his greatest scientific theories. Otto Hahn (1879–1968), the man who discovered atomic fission, was born just six days before Einstein. Also in 1879, Thomas Edison (1847–1931) and Joseph Swan (1828–1914) independently invented the incandescent light bulb. The same year saw the publication of Heinrich von Treitschke's *German History in the Nineteenth Century*, which proposed the fateful theory that it was Prussia's destiny to lead a united Germany. Born in the decade of German unification, Einstein lived to see the German nation defeated in two world wars and finally split into two countries. Treitschke, Professor of History at Berlin University where Einstein would eventually work, made no secret of his hostility towards the Jews. Indeed, in the year of Einstein's birth the term 'anti-Semitism' was coined by Wilhelm Marr. After the disastrous banking crash of 1873, Germany embarked on a course of industrial expansion under its iron chancellor, Otto von Bismarck (1815–98). By the beginning of the First World War Germany would have the most powerful economy in Europe.

Industrialisation led to an exodus from the countryside to the towns. Between 1870 and 1900, the number of Jews living in rural areas fell by 70 per cent. Numbered among these statistics was

Einstein's father, Hermann, who was born 30 August 1847 in the small town of Buchau on Lake Feder, some 30 miles south-west of Ulm. He had a sister and five brothers, one of whom died in infancy. His family could trace their ancestors back to the arrival in Buchau of one Baruch Moises Ainstein in 1665. Einsteins lived in

Hermann Einsten and Pauline Koch

Ulm until 1968, when Albert's great-nephew Siegbert (a survivor of the Theresienstadt concentration camp) died. Maria, Albert's younger sister (known in the family as Maja), says that their father 'showed a marked inclination for mathematics', but his family could not afford a university education.[6] 'Perhaps,' suggests Maja in the biographical sketch of her brother that she started in 1924, 'this very potential, left fallow in the father, developed all the more strongly in his son Albert.'[7] In 1866 the family moved to Ulm and Hermann became an apprentice in his cousin's feather bedding firm.

Just before his 29th birthday in 1876, Hermann Einstein married the 18-year-old Pauline Koch. Her family lived in the town of Cannstatt, near Stuttgart, where her father, Julius Koch, ran an extremely successful grain-trading business together with his brother Heinrich. 'The brothers and their families,' writes Maja, 'shared a single household under the same roof. Their wives shared the cooking, each taking charge of and responsibility for it in weekly turns. If such an arrangement is rather rare ... theirs was all the more remarkable because it lasted for decades without the least friction.'[8] Pauline's family was wealthy, and she was well educated; it seemed that their future together promised to be both 'carefree' and 'very prosperous'.[9] But it was not to be.

Maja describes her mother as a practical woman with a 'warm and caring nature'. Although her 'feelings were seldom given free rein' her grey eyes were often lit with a 'waggish twinkle'. She was 'accustomed to an opulent household', but her marriage meant that 'she learned early about the realities of life'.[10] Pauline played the piano well and passed her love of music on to her son. Perhaps she also gave him her 'perseverance and patience',[11] for when asked what made a good theoretical physicist, Einstein replied, *Patience! Then a little more patience.*[12]

Hermann's character also reveals traits that can be seen in his son. Maja mentions his 'contemplative nature' and his 'particularly pronounced way of trying to get to the bottom of something, by examining it from every side'.[13] Hermann was also a kind and generous man, 'endowed with an unfailing goodness of heart, a well-meaning nature that could refuse nothing to anyone'.[14] When he became famous, his son would reveal a similar generosity and an instinctive sympathy for the underdog. Indeed, his second wife Elsa often complained that he was a soft touch for beggars. But these admirable qualities did not serve Hermann well in the world of business. He was, says historian Fritz Stern, 'an amiable failure, mildly inept at all the businesses he started'.[15]

In June 1880 the Einsteins moved to Munich, the capital of Bavaria. Though a deeply conservative city, Munich also prided itself on being the 'cultural capital of Germany', as it was described in 1889.[16] Munich was a beguiling mixture of conservative tradition and bohemian excess, and in the *fin-de-siècle* period it became the centre of *Jugendstil*, the German version of art nouveau. In 1894 the novelist Thomas Mann (1875–1955) left northern Germany to live in Schwabing, a quarter of Munich described by his brother Viktor as 'Munich's Montparnasse' and home to many avant-garde artists, writers, musicians, and actors.[17] In 1911, the expressionist art movement *Der Blaue Reiter* (The Blue Rider) was born in Munich, attracting young artists such as Paul Klee.

Einstein grew up in this city of the arts, living here for 14 years. His father had entered into business with his younger brother Jakob,

'Munich was radiant. Above the gay squares and white columned temples, the classicist monuments and the baroque churches, the leaping fountains, the palaces and parks of the Residence there stretched a sky of luminous blue silk [. . .] Many windows stood open and music was heard from within: practising on piano, cello, or violin – earnest and well-meant amateur efforts; while from the Odeon came the sound of serious work on several grand pianos [. . .] Art flourished, art swayed the destinies of the town, art stretched above it her rose-bound sceptre and smiled. On every hand obsequious interest was displayed in her prosperity, on every

hand she was served with industry and devotion. There was a downright cult of line, decoration, form, significance, beauty. Munich was radiant.'

THOMAS MANN, 'Gladius Dei' (1902)[18]

who ran a gas-fitting and plumbing firm in Munich. Born in 1850, Jakob Einstein was the only one of the brothers to enjoy the benefits of higher education, having studied engineering. He was an ambitious and talented inventor who was always bursting with enthusiasm for his new projects. Maja says he 'exerted a certain intellectual influence on Albert while he was growing up'.[19] But Hermann and Jakob were far from ideal business partners. A very different character from the slow and methodical Hermann, the 'highly imaginative' Jakob was 'an impetuous optimist [who] never understood how to deal with realities' and was 'unable to learn from any failure'. Hermann 'could refuse nothing to anyone' and so 'gave in to him out of sheer good nature before he was himself able to reach decisions in his business deliberations'.[20] The qualities that later endeared Albert Einstein to the world were a fatal weakness in his father.

'It was a time,' writes Maja, 'when all the world was beginning to install electric lighting.'[21] The leading figure in Germany's burgeoning electrical industry was Ernst Werner von Siemens (1816–92), who

The history of electricity

1746 Leyden jars invented by Pieter van Musschenbroek in Holland; an early form of capacitor which allows electric charge to be stored and transported.

1751 The word 'electrician' first used in print by Benjamin Franklin.

1752 Benjamin Franklin proves that lightning is an electrical phenomenon with his famous kite experiment in Philadelphia. Atmospheric electricity is conducted down the wet string of the kite and charges a Leyden jar. This leads to the invention of the lightning conductor.

1791 Luigi Galvani, *Commentary on the Effects of Electricity on Muscular Motion*. Galvani is the first person to investigate animal electricity after noticing the twitching in dissected frogs' legs caused by an electrical machine.

1800 Alessandro Volta announces the first electric battery, made of piles of alternate plates of silver and zinc. It produces the first reliable source of significant electric current and represents a crucial moment in the history of physics.

1820 Hans Christian Oersted discovers the link between electricity and magnetism. He demonstrates that the magnetic effect of electric current flowing in a conducting wire is motion, a discovery that leads to the invention of the motor.

1831 Michael Faraday discovers electromagnetic induction, the creation of electricity by magnetism. Faraday produces a current by moving a magnet through a closed coil of wire. This leads to the invention of the first electric generator the following year. Faraday shows that electricity, magnetism, and mechanical motion

in 1867 had invented a revolutionary dynamo (a machine that generates high intensity current) that heralded a new age of affordable electric lighting and power. As already noted, the incandescent light bulb was invented in the same year Einstein was born and soon New York's streets were illuminated by this new technology. The electrotechnical industry was still an intensely competitive market, with many small to medium-sized firms vying for business. In Germany in 1890 there were 15,000 electrical workers; eight years later this figure had risen to 54,417. At the end of the 19th century, as far as electrification was concerned, Munich was lagging behind Berlin, where Siemens was based.

Initially Hermann became a partner in the firm Jakob Einstein &

are linked. In the 1830s and 1840s he develops the idea of an electrical or magnetic field created by 'lines of force' between charged particles (which can be seen in the patterns of iron filings around a magnet). Faraday directs attention away from magnets and wires to the space around them, and thereby to the electromagnetic field that Maxwell will later describe.

1837 Charles Wheatstone invents the first electric telegraph and Samuel Morse develops his alphabetic code of dots and dashes.

1854 London and Paris connected by telegraph.

1857–8 First trans-Atlantic telegraph cable.

1864 In his *Dynamical Theory of the Electromagnetic Field*, James Clerk Maxwell translates Faraday's qualitative descriptions of the electromagnetic field into mathematics in the form of wave equations. Maxwell's equations explains the propagation of electrical and magnetic forces across the whole spectrum from gamma waves to radio waves and shows that light too is electromagnetic radiation.

1867 Ernst Werner von Siemens announces a revolutionary dynamo that will herald a 'new era in electromagnetism'. Cheap electric lighting and power will be the result.

1879 Thomas Edison in America and Joseph Swan in England independently invent the incandescent light bulb.

1887–8 Heinrich Hertz confirms Maxwell's prediction that electromagnetic waves could be transmitted and discovers radio waves.

1895 Guglielmo Marconi develops wireless telegraphy.

1901 First radio transmission across the Atlantic.

Co, taking over the commercial side of things. In 1882 the brothers bought a two-thirds interest in Ludwig Kiessling & Co. That year they exhibited dynamos, arc and incandescent lights, and even a telephone system at the Munich International Electrical Exhibition. In May 1885 Hermann and Jakob entered the competitive field of electrical power generation and opened a factory, the Elektro-Technische Fabrik J Einstein & Co, at 125 Lindwurmstrasse. As one of their first contracts they had the honour of supplying electric lighting for Munich's Oktoberfest – the first time the annual beer-drinking festival had been lit by electricity. It is likely they used one of the dynamos designed by Jakob, the firm's technical wizard. From 1886 to 1893, Jakob took out six patents for improved arc lamps, a circuit-breaker, and instruments for measuring electric currents. At first the firm did well and the factory had to be expanded after they won several big contracts installing power plants and lighting systems. Their greatest success came in 1888 with the contract to supply power and lighting to Schwabing. In 1891, at the height of the firm's success, they took part in Germany's biggest exhibition of electrotechnology at Frankfurt. Modelled on the immensely popular world fairs, the event attracted over a million paying visitors and even the Kaiser toured the grounds.

J Einstein & Co was small, employing fewer than 200 people, and to survive in an increasingly competitive market it needed capital, and lots of it. Cash-flow problems hit the firm in 1892. As well as Pauline's substantial dowry, her father Julius Koch (who lived with the Einsteins after his wife's death in 1886) contributed significant sums to the firm. But it was not enough. By 1893 Hermann and Jakob had taken out about 60,000 marks in bank loans, guaranteed against their home at 14 Adlzreiterstrasse. That year the Nuremberg firm Schuckert & Co secured the street lighting contract for Munich. It was the final blow. Hermann and Jakob had banked everything on winning the contract and the firm was wound up in July 1894.

It was a traumatic period for Albert and his family. An Italian representative of the firm, Lorenzo Garrone, suggested they re-locate the business to northern Italy and the impulsive Jakob had soon convinced Hermann this was a good idea. In the meantime the garden of their Munich home was sold to a property developer to pay debts and finance the move. In July building work began and Maja recalled how they watched their beloved garden turned into a construction site, 'the magnificent old trees' felled to make way for 'an entire row of ugly apartment houses'.[22] Both families had lived together in the comfortable villa in the Adlzreiterstrasse, echoing the unconventional living arrangements of Pauline's parents. Albert lived here for nine happy years, growing up in an affluent, bourgeois environment. The extended family of Kochs and Einsteins were frequent visitors, including his cousin Elsa, the daughter of Pauline's sister, Fanny.

A biography by Einstein's stepson-in-law, Rudolf Kayser, described the 'well-to-do philistine atmosphere' of the Einstein family home.[23] As an adult, Einstein rejected what he saw as the materialistic values of his parents, but there is no doubt that the environment in which he grew up was full of stimulation – music, literature, and science were ever-present: Pauline was a talented pianist and music was to became one of Einstein's great pleasures in life. His father would often read the poems of Heinrich Heine (1797–1856) to his family and the German poet remained one of Einstein's favourites. Jakob was always keen to interest his nephew in the wonders of the latest technology and played a vital role in encouraging Einstein's interest in physics and mathematics. Indeed, throughout his life Einstein enjoyed applying his scientific knowledge to practical problems. In 1908 he invented an instrument for measuring extremely small voltages (below 0.0005 volts), which he later patented. In the 1920s he worked with Hungarian physicist Leo Szilard (1898–1964) to develop an innovative pump for household refrigerators. Such inventive ability owes much to his uncle Jakob, and the science of electricity was to play a major role in Einstein's life and work.

Carl Seelig, one of Einstein's early biographers, once asked him whether he inherited his scientific abilities from his father or mother. Einstein's reply was dismissive: *I have no particular talent, I am merely extremely inquisitive. So I think we can dispense with this question of heritage.*[24] He claimed that it was *curiosity, obsession, and sheer perseverance that brought me to my ideas,* not inheritance or upbringing.[25] In fact Einstein was extremely reluctant to discuss his childhood, or indeed his personal life. His sister Maja's unfinished biography is virtually the only inside view we have of life in the Einstein family. He was eventually cajoled into writing a brief life history in 1946, but this intellectual autobiography affords us scant insight into the man behind the science. As if to discourage biographers, he stated *what is essential in the life of a man of my kind is what he thinks and how he thinks, and not what he does or suffers.*[26] From an early age Einstein says he longed to free himself from the *chains of the 'merely personal', from an existence dominated by wishes, hopes, and primitive feelings.*[27] The objectivity of scientific knowledge offered him this freedom, but the flight from the merely personal runs like a red thread throughout Einstein's life. His dedication to science resulted in a feeling of isolation and he once said: *I have never belonged full-heartedly to a country, a State, nor to a circle of friends, nor even to my own family.*[28]

Einstein was a quiet, dreamy child who kept to himself. He was certainly no *Wunderkind* and for a time his parents, who feared their 'pathologically modest'[29] child might have learning difficulties, even consulted a doctor. But his maternal grandmother, Jette Koch, was delighted by Einstein's 'droll ideas'.[30] Maja describes one of these: 'When the two year old was told of the arrival of a little sister with whom he could play, he imagined a kind of toy, for at the sight of this new creature he asked, with great disappointment: *Yes, but where are its wheels?*'[31] The new sister was Maja, Einstein's only sibling, born in November 1881. She recalls that even as a boy, when asked a question her brother would repeat it to himself 'softly, moving his lips'.[32] For the maidservant this indicated stupidity, but to the more sympathetic Maja 'thoroughness in thinking'.[33] Einstein even attributed his scientific insight to this slow development, a fact that will no doubt reassure many parents: *The normal adult never bothers his head about space–time problems. Everything there is to be thought about it, in his opinion, has already been done in early childhood. I, on the contrary, developed so slowly that I only began to wonder about space and time when I was already grown up. In consequence I probed deeper into the problem than an ordinary child would have done.*[34]

Perhaps because of the continuing concerns of Einstein's parents for their shy and pensive boy, they were keen to give him self-confidence. Maja tells how the three- or four-year-old Einstein was 'sent through the busiest streets of Munich', at first with Pauline, but then alone, or rather 'unobtrusively observed'. It seems he was not at all frightened and 'at intersections he conscientiously looked right, then left, and then crossed the road without any apprehension.'[35] Biographers Roger Highfield and Paul Carter suggest that Pauline 'was less interested in showering her son with love than in making sure he developed more backbone than his father'.[36] She was certainly the dominant figure in the Einstein household. When he was once asked who was the head of his family, Einstein's reply was a terse *cannot be answered*. He was quick to assert his father's *good humour, patience, goodness, charm*, but less forthcoming about his mother's qualities.[37] When questioned about her secret of running a successful household, Pauline replied with a smile: 'Discipline.'[38]

When he was five, Einstein's parents hired a private tutor. Unfortunately, she provoked one of the boy's infamous temper tantrums during which 'he grabbed a chair and struck at his teacher, who was so frightened that she ran away terrified and was never seen again.'[39] Maja herself fell victim to these rages and on one occasion he attempted to 'knock a hole in her head' with a child's hoe.[40] Although these temper tantrums disappeared during his schooling, Maja speaks from painful experience when she says 'it takes a sound skull to be the sister of an intellectual'.[41] It was at this early age that Einstein's violin lessons began, continuing until the age of 14. At first he disliked the endless repetitive practice, but eventually music became a vital

The six-year-old Albert Einstein with his sister Maja

DISCIPLINE

part of his life. He later wrote that it was only after he had *fallen in love* with Mozart's sonatas at the age of 13 that he truly began to understand and appreciate music. He added that *love is a better teacher than duty*, a statement that was undoubtedly true for Einstein who always hated mechanical approaches to education.[42] For Maja there was no doubt that his musical gift came from his mother's side of the family and his 'mathematical and logical' abilities from his father's.[43] It was to prove a remarkably creative mix of talents.

Science and music entered Einstein's life at the same time. While he was recovering in bed from an illness, his father gave him a pocket compass to play with. Einstein was fascinated by the movement of the needle, which obeyed an invisible and mysterious force to always point north. More than half a century later, he recalled the episode, using it to show how a childlike sense of wonder plays a key role in understanding the world: *I can still remember [. . .] that this experience made a deep and lasting impression upon me. Something deeply hidden had to be behind things. What man sees before him from infancy causes no reaction of this kind; he is not surprised by the falling of bodies, by wind and rain, nor by the moon, nor by the fact that the moon does not fall down, nor by the differences between living and nonliving matter.*[45] For Einstein, the adult intellect was engaged in a *continuous flight from 'wonder'.*[46] Although he himself inhabited a realm of pure thought, he never forgot the importance of this instinctive, childlike wonder as a source of inspiration: *The most beautiful experience we can have is the mysterious. It is the fundamental*

Einstein had a deep love of music that verged on the spiritual. Hans Byland recalls playing Mozart sonatas with the 17-year-old Einstein: 'When he began to play his violin, the room seemed to broaden out. For the first time I was listening to the real Mozart in all the Grecian beauty of its clear lines, alternately graceful and magnificently powerful. *That is heavenly*, he said, *we must play it again*. What fire there was in his playing! I no longer recognised him.' Einstein's favourite composers were Bach, Mozart, and Schubert; he was less keen on Handel and Beethoven. When asked by a newspaper about Bach he replied: *What I have to say of Bach's life work? Listen, play, love, revere and . . . keep your mouth shut.*[44]

emotion which stands at the cradle of true art and true science. Whoever does not know it and can no longer wonder, no longer marvel, is as good as dead, and his eyes are dimmed.[47] In this sense, Einstein's love of music and science complemented each other and were *nourished by the same sort of longing.*[48]

Einstein began primary school in autumn 1885. The Roman Catholic Petersschule in nearby Blumenstrasse was a large school of some 2,000 pupils. Out of the 70 children in Einstein's class he was the only Jew. During one of the religious studies lessons the teacher produced a large nail and told his class that 'with just such nails Christ had been nailed to the Cross by the Jews'.[49] At this time, Einstein also recalls being the victim of racial taunts: *Physical attacks and insults on the way home from school were frequent, but mostly not too vicious. They were sufficient, however, to confirm even in a child a lively sense of being an outsider.*[50] This quiet boy, who never liked sports or taking part in the games of other children, was not popular and soon earned the nick-name *Biedermeier* ('nerd' or 'goody-goody'). Despite having a mathematics teacher who believed in regularly administered raps on the knuckles, Einstein was soon 'top of his class and has got a brilliant report', as his mother proudly told his sister.[51]

Aged nine and a half Einstein entered Munich's prestigious Luitpold Gymnasium, a secondary school that offered its pupils a classical education, teaching Latin and Greek. According to science historian Lewis Pyenson it was unusual for 'a manufacturer's son' to attend 'the elite and expensive Luitpold Gymnasium'.[52] A photograph of Einstein's class in 1889 shows the young Einstein third from the right in the front row. He is the only one of his class to have a broad grin on his face. But appearances are often deceptive, as Einstein's scientific theories would suggest. He was not at all happy at the Gymnasium: *The teachers at the elementary school seemed to me like drill sergeants,* he later commented, *and the teachers at the Gymansium like lieutenants.*[53] Throughout his life, Einstein disapproved of educational methods based on *drill, external authority, and ambition.*[54] He was not alone. A young generation of writers, including Hesse and Thomas Mann, would soon criticise the harsh and regimented education system in Germany.

However, in comparison to other schools in Germany (particularly the Prussian north), Munich's schools were relatively liberal. Under its headmaster, Dr Wolfgang Markhausen, the Luitpold Gymnasium was regarded as an 'enlightened school'.[55] It was large, with some 684 pupils in 1888 when Einstein joined, rising to 1,330 when he left in 1894. Only 5 per cent of the school's mainly Catholic pupils were Jewish, although this was a larger proportion than in the population of Munich as a whole. Einstein's mathematics teacher, Adolf Sickenberger, was extremely gifted and regarded as progressive in his approach to teaching. But before the young Einstein discovered the joys of mathematics, he found religion.

For a year or so after starting at the Luitpold Gymnasium, Einstein turned to the Jewish faith with a fervency that must have unsettled his parents. In his own words he was *the child of entirely irreligious (Jewish) parents.*[56] Hermann and Pauline were assimilated, liberal Jews: they did not observe the Hebrew rituals, their home was not kosher and Hermann preferred reading his Swabian countryman

When I was a fairly precocious young man I became thoroughly impressed with the futility of the hopes and strivings that chase most men restlessly through life. Moreover, I soon discovered the cruelty of that chase, which in those years was much more carefully covered up by hypocrisy and glittering words than is the case today. By the mere existence of his stomach everyone was condemned to participate in that chase. The stomach might well be satisfied by such participation, but not man insofar as he is a thinking and feeling being. As the first way out there was religion, which is implanted into every child by way of the traditional education-machine.[58]

Friedrich Schiller (1759–1805) than the Talmud. While at the Luitpold, however, young Einstein was taught about Judaism and, according to Maja, 'a deep religious feeling was awakened in him.'[57] He gave up eating pork and even composed songs praising God which he would sing on the way to school. His parents watched his conversion in bemused silence, but Einstein's *deep religiousness* was short-lived, ending at the age of 12.[59] He never again believed in a personal god, a notion he described as *naïve*.[60] He did not even become bar mitzvah. Like Karl Marx (1818–83), Einstein came to view religion as an opiate whose function was to numb people's senses to the soul-destroying monotony of their daily lives and to prevent them from questioning the status quo. He emerged from the *religious paradise of youth* feeling angry and believing that *youth is intentionally being deceived by the State through lies.*[61] It was science and mathematics that opened his eyes to the real world. *If something is in me that can be called religious,* he wrote just before his death, *then it is the unbounded admiration for the structure of the world so far as our science can reveal it.*[62]

Traditionally in Jewish homes the Sabbath lunch is shared with a needy Talmudic scholar. Not keen to encourage their son's religiosity, Einstein's parents chose to invite a medical student from Munich University. From 1889 the 21-year-old Max Talmud visited every week (on Thursday, rather than the Sabbath) and soon became close friends with the young Einstein. He encouraged his interest in science, introducing him to such classic works as Alexander von Humboldt's *Kosmos* (1845–62), the last flowering of German Romantic science, and Ludwig Büchner's *Force and Matter* (1855), the bible of German materialism in the 19th century. Talmud also recommended that the 13-year-old Einstein should read Kant's *Critique of Pure Reason* (1781). The

In his famous *Critique of Pure Reason* (1781), German philosopher Immanuel Kant (1724–1804) explores the limited means by which humankind interprets experience.

Enlightenment philosopher's ideas, together with those of physicist and philosopher Ernst Mach (1838–1916), would show Einstein that time and space (those unchallengeable absolutes of Newtonian physics) were not universal realities but variable concepts. Talmud also lent him Aaron Bernstein's *Popular Books on Natural Science* (1853–7), a 20-volume survey of the course of science. This was like manna from heaven for Einstein and he read them with *breathless attention.*[63] According to Einstein scholars Jürgen Renn and Robert

Schulmann, 'the topics treated by Bernstein contain striking parallels to some of Einstein's ideas'.[64] The link between molecular forces and gravitation, the corpuscular theory of light and even the possibility that light might be affected by gravitational fields were subjects Bernstein covered and which in coming years his young reader, Albert Einstein, would completely revolutionise.

By the time he met Talmud, Einstein had already been initiated into the wonders of mathematics. His uncle Jakob had explained Pythagoras's theorem that the square of the hypotenuse on a right-angled triangle is equal to the sum of the squares of the other two sides. Einstein was so fascinated by this that he spent the next three weeks putting it to the test. Jakob had also introduced his nephew to algebra, telling him that it was a 'merry science in which we go hunting for a little animal whose name we don't know. So we call it *x*. When we bag the game we give it the right name.'[65]

The Greek philosopher Pythagoras (sixth century BC) probably discovered the geometrical theorem named after him and certainly discovered the arithmetical ratios governing musical intervals, which led him to interpret the universe in terms of mathematics alone.

At the age of 12 Einstein had discovered what he called *a holy little book of geometry*.[66] It was probably the *Textbook of Elementary Mathematics* (1888) written by Einstein's own maths teacher, Sickenberger, part of which dealt with Euclidean plane geometry. 'Play and playmates were forgotten' as Einstein sat alone working his way through this book.[67] Its *lucidity and certainty made an indescribable impression on me*, he wrote.[68] Philosopher Bertrand Russell (1872–1970), who helped popularise the theory of relativity, was similarly impressed by Euclid at the age of 11, describing it as 'one of the great events of my life, as dazzling as first love'.[69] For Einstein, it was a model of pure thought. *If Euclid failed to kindle your youthful enthusiasm*, he wrote later, *then you were not born to be a scientific thinker*.[70] But his new-found scepticism meant that he had to spend three weeks strenuously testing its logical rigour to the best of his ability. The truth of the axioms or basic statements of Euclidean geometry had stood the test of time. And yet the adult Einstein's general theory of relativity would show that a far more complex and subtle geometry than that used by the ancient Greeks was needed to describe the universe.

In his book *Elements* the Greek mathematician Euclid (*c.*300BC) summarised all known geometry from a few simple rules. Geometry obeying Euclid's rules is called Euclidean, while all other kinds are non-Euclidean.

From the age of 12 Einstein excelled at mathematics. In science and mathematics he found a new wonder against which religion paled into insignificance. He also did well in Latin and Greek, but his Greek teacher, Dr Joseph Degenhart, was unimpressed and told Einstein that 'nothing would ever become of him.'[71] He also accused Einstein of undermining his respect in the class, for the independently minded Einstein resented all authority. The solitary, bookish boy appeared aloof and even potentially rebellious to his teachers.

By the time Einstein entered Degenhart's class, dramatic changes had taken place at home. The family firm had failed and the Einsteins had decided to relocate to Milan. The 15-year-old Albert had to stay in a boarding house in Munich to complete the final three years of his schooling, but away from his family he became deeply unhappy. Einstein's 'laconically phrased' letters to his parents in Milan gave no clue to his 'depressed and nervous' state.[72] After six months of solitude the teenager visited Max's brother, Bernard Talmud, a Munich doctor who sympathised with Einstein's plight and gave him a medical certificate excusing him from school on health grounds. Einstein's maths teacher also provided a letter attesting to his excellent mathematical abilities.

Einstein could not leave Germany fast enough. Whether it was the *dull and mechanical method of teaching*[73] or the *over-emphasised military mentality*,[74] it is impossible to say. Certainly the prospect of serving in the German army, which was obligatory at the age of 20, filled the free-thinking and anti-authoritarian Einstein with absolute 'dread'.[75] Whatever the reason, his parents were shocked when he suddenly turned up in Milan at the end of December 1894. They knew only too well that without his school leaving certificate, Albert would not be able to attend university in Germany. The young man who was destined to change the course of modern science did not have a propitious beginning: at the age of 15 he was a school drop-out.

A studio portrait of the fourteen-year-old Einstein when he was a scholar in Munich, 1893

The Relentlessly Strict Angels
1894–1900

Hermann and Jakob founded their new firm, Società Einstein, Garrone e Cia, on 14 March 1894, Albert's 15th birthday. By October they were living in a spacious apartment at Via Berchet 2, near Milan's fine 14th-century cathedral. But what probably impressed the young Einstein more when he arrived was the Galleria Vittorio Emanuele II, known as 'the drawing room of Milan', because of its many cafés. Completed a year before Einstein was born, it was among the first buildings in Europe to use iron and glass as structural features. Just a stone's throw from Einstein's apartment, it was an impressive symbol of Italy's industrial and technological confidence at the end of the 19th century.

While in Munich, the Einstein family firm had already installed electricity supply systems in the small north Italian towns of Varese and Susa. By moving to a region that contained most of Italy's chemical and manufacturing plants, Hermann and Jakob hoped to find new opportunities. It was a brave decision, but unfortunately it did not pay off. With financial backing from Hermann's cousin, Rudolf Einstein, a wealthy Swabian textile manufacturer, they built an electrical factory in the small university town of Pavia, where the inventor of the electric battery, Alessandro Volta (1745–1827), had taught physics a century earlier. But when they failed to win a contract to supply electricity to Pavia in October 1895, they once again faced liquidation and heavy losses. This time Jakob had learnt his lesson and went to work for an Italian engineering firm. He later moved to Vienna, where he died in 1912.

The Galleria Vittorio Emanuele II in Milan

Hermann soldiered on, starting yet another electrotechnical firm against the advice of his son. Maja explains that her father 'did not want to bring suffering on his wife, who would have had great difficulty accommodating herself to any lower standing in the social scale.'[76] Despite their losses they moved back to Milan into an 11-room apartment at Via Bigli 21. Within a couple of years Hermann's new business had also folded with heavy losses. Writing to his sister in 1898, Einstein revealed his anxiety at this time: *If things had gone my way, Papa would have looked for employment already two years ago, and he and we would have been spared the worst . . . What depresses me most is, of course, the misfortune of my poor parents who have not had a happy moment for so many years. What further hurts me deeply is that, as an adult, I have to look on without being able to do anything. After all, I am nothing but a burden to my family . . . It would be better if I were not alive at all.*[77]

When Einstein unexpectedly turned up in December 1894, his parents were certainly worried that he might become a burden. He tried to reassure them with plans for a career teaching philosophy, but Hermann and Pauline were distinctly unimpressed by this 'philosophical nonsense'.[78] Despite Hermann's unhappy experiences, it was agreed that Einstein should follow a career in electrical engineering. As he could not attend a German university without a school leaving certificate, his parents decided he should apply to the Swiss Federal Polytechnical Institute in German-speaking Zurich, which accepted students on completion of an entrance examination. With characteristic self-confidence, Einstein insisted on preparing himself for the exam in autumn 1895. Maja recalls how at this time 'even in a large, quite noisy group, he could withdraw to the sofa, take pen and paper in hand, set the inkstand precariously on the armrest, and lose himself so completely in a problem' that he was soon unaware of what was happening around him, an ability that Einstein retained throughout his life.[79]

Although Einstein spent the spring and summer of 1895 travelling in northern Italy, evidence of his studies can be seen in a short essay he sent to his favourite uncle, Caesar Koch. 'On the Investigation of the State of the Ether in a Magnetic Field' is Einstein's first scientific essay. It follows contemporary thinking, which viewed electric and magnetic fields as states of the ether (an invisible substance that was believed to fill all space and which Einstein himself later rejected), but it is undoubtedly an impressive piece of work for a 16-year-old. Quite what his uncle, a grain merchant in Brussels, made of it we do not know. Passages in the essay also bear more than a passing resemblance to an article published a few years earlier in a popular science journal.[80] But the subject testifies to Einstein's fascination with electrical and magnetic phenomena that began at the age of five with his father's compass.

Einstein also helped his uncle Jakob with electrical design work. Jakob liked to tell friends how he and his engineer had been puzzling for days over the calculations for a machine they were constructing. Einstein took barely 15 minutes to come up with the solution and his proud uncle predicted his nephew would go far.

Entrants to the Zurich Polytechnic were usually 18 and its director, Albin Herzog, allowed Einstein to take the examination only when he was told that the 16-year-old was a 'child prodigy'.[81] But Einstein did not live up to expectations and failed. Nevertheless, his performance in the scientific part of the exam was impressive enough for the physics professor, Heinrich Friedrich Weber, to invite him to attend his lectures – an unusual honour which must have softened the blow.

Einstein had to accept the inevitable and return to school. Herzog recommended one in the Swiss town of Aarau, 50 kilometres from

Zurich, just half an hour by train. Einstein was pleasantly surprised by the Swiss approach to education. The ethos of the school was inspired by Swiss educational reformer Johann Heinrich Pestalozzi (1746–1827) who emphasised the importance of students developing their own individual understanding of the world. Founded in 1802, it was one of the finest schools in Switzerland and Einstein described it as *an unforgettable oasis in that European oasis, Switzerland.*[82] He enrolled at the school at the end of October 1895 and spent a year there, along with his cousin Robert Koch. The school was divided into a Gymnasium and a technical school where Einstein studied. The head of the school and Einstein's physics tutor was August Tuchschmid, who was proud of the school's pupil-centred approach to learning. The standard of science teaching was excellent. Indeed, Einstein was not the only former pupil to win a Nobel Prize for science: Paul Karrer (1889–1971) won the 1937 prize for chemistry.

According to Maja this was one of the best periods in her brother's life.[83] Never keen on big cities, Einstein felt instantly at ease in the small-town atmosphere of Aarau. He lodged with the family of Jost Winteler, who taught classics at the school, a subject Einstein no longer needed to study. He soon felt at home with the Wintelers, even calling them Mama and Papa.[84] He joined the family on their regular walks and made kites for their seven children. Relieved that his wilful son was finally on the road to a secure future, Hermann Einstein thanked Jost Winteler with heartfelt gratitude for looking after Albert and for the 'many intellectual benefits his stay there is going to bring him'.[85]

Einstein was a year younger than his classmates, one of whom, Hans Byland, later described him as an 'impudent Swabian': 'Sure of himself, his grey felt hat pushed back on his thick, black hair, he strode energetically up and down in the rapid, I might almost say crazy, tempo of a restless spirit which carries a whole world in itself. Nothing escaped the sharp gaze of his large bright brown eyes. Whoever approached him immediately came under the spell of his superior personality. A sarcastic curl of his rather full mouth with the protruding lower lip did not encourage Philistines to fraternise with him. Unhampered by convention, his attitude towards the world was that of a laughing philosopher and his witty mockery pitilessly lashed any conceit or pose.'[86] This romanticised picture portrays an outspoken, self-confident young man, whose sharp tongue protected an 'intense emotional life' which found expression through his love of music.[87] Indeed, in March 1896 a music examiner singled Einstein out for particular praise: 'One student, by the name of Einstein, even sparkled by rendering an adagio from a Beethoven sonata with deep understanding.'[88] He gained a reputation for being a 'lone wolf' and a 'gypsy', phrases Einstein adopted in his letters.[89] As in Munich, his self-assurance was sometimes interpreted as arrogance or even rudeness, something that was to cause him problems with lecturers at the Zurich Polytechnic. One Aarau classmate recalled a field trip with their natural history teacher, Professor Fritz Mühlberg, who asked, 'Now, Einstein, how do the strata run here? From below upwards or vice versa?' To which came the cheeky response: *It is pretty much the same to me whichever way they run, Professor.*[90]

Einstein learnt much during his year at Aarau, not least from Mühlberg, an admirer of Alexander von Humboldt, whose *Kosmos* Einstein knew well. Like other teachers at the school, Mühlberg aimed at fostering in his pupils a desire to 'advance knowledge' and to 'discover the truth', believing that concepts, theories and fundamental laws were more important in science than the encyclopaedic accumulation of facts.[91] It was a view Einstein made his own. These enlightened educational methods clearly inspired Einstein for here he first began exploring ideas that were to lead to his theory of relativity. What would you see, he wondered, if you could keep pace with a wave of light? But he would have to wait nine years for the answer to this *Gedankenexperiment* or 'thought experiment'.

The adolescent Einstein developed emotionally as well as intellectually at Aarau. He fell in love with Jost's daughter, 18-year-old Marie

THE STUDENT

Winteler. A letter from Einstein to Marie, written during the Easter holidays in 1896, reveals their love: *It is so wonderful to be able to press to one's heart such a bit of paper which two so dear little eyes have lovingly beheld and on which the dainty little hands have charmingly glided back and forth.*[92] In his love letters Einstein slips easily into kitschy sentiment: she was his *beloved, naughty little angel* and only now did he realise *how indispensable my dear little sunshine has become to my happiness.*[93] He is keen to win his mother's approval for their relationship and shows her Marie's letters: *My mother has also taken you to her heart. [. . .] Moreover, she always laughs at me because I am no longer attracted to the girls who were supposed to have enchanted me so much in the past.*[94] Clearly the 'gypsy' Einstein, with his dark curly hair and violin, was no stranger to the ladies. According to friend and biographer Antonina Vallentin, 'as a young man and even in middle age, Einstein had regular features, plump cheeks, a round chin – masculine good looks of the type that played havoc at the turn of the century.' With his 'dark, compelling' eyes, 'generous mouth' and 'muscular body' he looked more like a romantic poet than a scientist.[95]

In September 1896 Einstein took his school leaving examinations. There were seven written papers as well as oral exams and Einstein

Graduation photograph of Einstein (seated on the left), Zurich Polytechnic, 1900

passed all with flying colours: his grade average was 5.5 out of a possible 6 – the highest in his class (he got full marks for algebra and geometry). They were more than sufficient to guarantee him a place at the Zurich Polytechnic. In a brief essay entitled 'My Plans for the Future', written for his French exam (his weakest subject), Einstein looks forward to studying maths and physics in Zurich with a view to eventually teaching them. Clearly, the wilful Einstein had no intention of following in his father's footsteps. But he had a surprisingly mature understanding of his own strengths and weaknesses, revealing that he wanted to study these subjects because of *my individual inclination for abstract and mathematical thinking, lack of imagination and of practical sense. [. . .] Besides, I am also much attracted by a certain independence offered by the scientific profession.*[96]

At the beginning of October, Einstein enrolled at the Zurich Polytechnic or Poly as it was known to the students. Marie Winteler was now teaching in the village of Olsberg, from where she wrote in November: 'My love, I do not quite understand a passage in your letter. You write that you do not want to correspond with me any longer, but why not, sweetheart?'[97] Einstein had decided to end their relationship and wanted to break the news gently. Her letter, in which she calls him her 'great dear philosopher' and 'darling curlyhead' ends almost pleadingly: 'I love you for all eternity.'[98] It was not what Einstein wanted to hear. In another letter she tells him that she wants to see 'where my darling dreams away his days' and announces that she intends to 'arrange everything the way I like it, and you will enjoy your little study room twice as much'.[99] It was the last straw for Einstein, who had rented a room at 4 Unionstrasse, Zurich. Marie had once described herself as the 'insignificant silly little sweetheart that knows nothing and understands nothing'.[100] In Aarau Einstein had denied this was the case, but now, in the intellectually challenging environment of Zurich, she seemed to be speaking to him from another world. He was happy to send Marie his dirty laundry, which she would walk an hour and a half to the station to collect, but he did not want her tidying his room. It is not clear if he formally broke off their relationship or simply stopped writing. A letter from Einstein's mother to Marie in December says he has become 'frightfully lazy' and 'the regularity of his letters leaves much to be desired'.[101]

Five months later, Einstein wrote a letter to Marie's mother – whom he addresses as *liebes Mamerl* ('dear mummy') – that gives us a rare insight into his character. He was declining an invitation to Aarau at Whitsun: *It would be more than unworthy of me to buy a few days of bliss at the cost of new pain, of which I have already caused much too much to the dear child through my fault.*[102] Marie was two years older than Einstein, but for him she was still a *child*, a description that reveals both the gulf between them and Einstein's attitude to women. As a result of their failed relationship, which both families hoped might lead to marriage, Marie suffered a breakdown. Einstein told her mother how he survived such emotional strains: *Strenuous intellectual work and looking at God's Nature are the reconciling, fortifying, yet relentlessly strict angels that shall lead me through all of life's troubles. If only I were able to give some of this to the good child! And yet, what a peculiar way this is to weather the storms of life – in many a lucid moment I appear to myself as an ostrich who buries his head in the desert sand so as not to perceive the danger. One creates a small little world for oneself, and as lamentably insignificant as it may be in comparison with the perpetually changing size of real existence, one feels miraculously great and important, just like a mole in his self-dug hole.*[103]

This uniquely revealing passage shows what became for Einstein a lifelong psychological opposition between *intellectual work* and the emotions. Science became a safe haven where Einstein could *weather the storms* in his personal life. In his relationship with Marie, as in others, including with his sons, Einstein showed a stubborn and even ruthless instinct for self-protection: his first loyalty was always to his intellectual work. He was swift to distance himself from emotional situations that he felt would endanger the peace of mind he needed to work. His confessional statement to Marie's mother is brutally honest and, for an 18-year-old, reveals an extraordinary degree of self-knowledge while admitting a certain emotional immaturity.

His closeness to Pauline Winteler is remarkable and one can scarcely imagine him writing such confessional letters to his own mother. He tells her that whenever he thinks of Aarau *his head starts ringing in a delightfully mad way*.[104] His existence in Zurich is by comparison *so philistine that people could use it for setting their watches – except that their watches would be somewhat late in the morning*.[105] There is no doubt that Einstein was *madly in love* with Marie,[106] a feeling that had still not subsided two years later. But by then he had fallen in love with one of his fellow students.

Opened in 1855, the Zurich Polytechnic where Einstein studied for four years had a reputation as one of the leading centres of mathematics and physics in German-speaking Europe. As a physics student, Einstein was enrolled in Department VI, the School for Specialised Teachers in Mathematical and Science Subjects. This was divided into two sections, B: Natural Sciences and A: Mathematics, with Einstein belonging to the latter. There were 841 students at the Poly when Einstein started in October 1896. At 17 and a half he was the youngest student. Of the four others who enrolled with him that year in Section VI A, Marcel Grossmann and Louis Kollros were 18, Jakob Ehrat (who joined in the second semester after

Marie Winteler (1877–1957) later said about Einstein: 'We loved each other deeply, but it was an entirely ideal love.'[107] After recovering from her breakdown, she taught at Murgenthal in the Aargau canton from 1902–5. In November 1906 tragedy struck the Winteler family. Pauline was shot and killed by her son Julius, a ship's cook, who had just returned from America. Before committing suicide he also murdered his sister Rosa's husband. Marie married Albert Müller in 1911. They had two sons but divorced in 1927 and Marie moved to Zurich where she gave music lessons and wrote poetry. In 1940 Einstein received two letters from Marie, asking if he could lend her money and help her emigrate to America. He never replied, though it is possible that his secretary did not show him the letters. Marie died in an asylum on 24 September 1957.

moving from Zurich University) was 20, and Mileva Marić – the only woman in the whole section – was 21. A student's course of study at the Poly was very flexible and Einstein took philosophy, politics, economics and geology options as well as ones on physics. To complete their studies they had to take an oral intermediate exam (Einstein took his in 1898) and then a final exam, which consisted of both an oral exam and a thesis, the *Diplomarbeit*. When Einstein finished his studies in July 1900 the Poly was still unable to grant doctorates (this changed in 1911), but students could submit a further thesis to Zurich University to qualify for a doctorate, as Einstein did in 1905.

Zurich was Switzerland's largest city and had emerged as the economic powerhouse of the country. During the First World War it would become home to émigrés such as Hermann Hesse, Vladimir Ilich Lenin (1870–1924), and James Joyce (1882–1941), as well as the writers and artists associated with the Dada movement. By 1896 the Einstein family firm had gone into liquidation again and money was short. While in Zurich, Einstein lived on an allowance of 100 Swiss francs a month from his wealthy Koch relatives in Genoa, supplemented by private tuition. He set aside 20 francs a month towards his future application for Swiss citizenship, having renounced his German nationality in January 1896. Indeed, until February 1901, when he became a Swiss citizen, Einstein was officially stateless.

Invented in Zurich in response to the carnage of the First World War, Dada was a precursor of Surrealism. Dadaists were anti-art and anti-sense, their main aim being to outrage and scandalise 'decent' opinion.

It was a modest amount, but certainly enough to live on. At the time you could rent a small, furnished room in Zurich for 20 francs a month, a better room with meals cost 70 francs. But Einstein was never interested in material things, saying once *the commonplace goals of human endeavour – possessions, outward success and luxury have always seemed to me despicable*.[108] Although he was not interested in following the beer-drinking ways of the popular student societies (*Beer makes a man stupid and lazy*, he said),[109] Einstein was a familiar face in the coffee houses along Bahnhofstrasse where he would sit lost in thought, surrounded by smoke from his pipe, a new-found pleasure.

Music played an important role in Einstein's student life. Susanne Markwalder, the daughter of his landlady at 87 Klosbachstrasse where Einstein lived during his third year, would accompany him on the piano. Once, hearing the sound of a Mozart piano sonata he burst into a neighbour's apartment: *Go on playing!* he said to the astonished pianist before joining in with his violin.[110] Einstein's only failing as a lodger was his habit of forgetting his keys. The bell would often ring in the middle of the night and Frau Markwalder would hear the cry: *It's Einstein! I've forgotten my keys again.*[111] On Lake Zurich Einstein discovered his love of sailing, often with Susanne, who remembered how when the wind dropped he would sometimes produce a notebook and begin hurriedly jotting down notes.

Music brought Einstein together with a man who was to play a vital role in his scientific work and become a life long friend. Michele Angelo Besso had transferred from Rome University to study engineering at the Poly, completing his studies in 1895. They met in 1897 during one of the many musical soirées at which Einstein played his violin. Throughout his life Einstein needed someone to act as a sounding board for his revolutionary scientific ideas and his conversations with Besso proved invaluable, especially during his work on relativity. Although he said that Besso had *an extraordinarily fine mind, whose working, though disorderly, I watch with great delight*, Einstein complained that Besso lacked his own single-minded dedication to science, describing him as *an awful weakling without a spark of healthy humaneness, who cannot rouse himself to any action in life or scientific creation.*[112] An intense, nervous man with an unkempt black beard, Besso married Anna Winteler, Marie's elder sister, in 1898.

Of the students in his year, Marcel Grossmann became a particularly close friend. He told his parents 'this Einstein will one day be a very great man'.[113] Unlike Einstein, Grossmann was a *model student* who attended lectures religiously and made copious notes that were very useful to Einstein when he was revising.[114] Einstein described himself as a *mediocre* student, only able to concentrate on subjects that interested him.[115]After a couple of semesters *I gradually learned to live with my guilty conscience and arranged my studies to suit my intellectual stomach and my interests. Some lectures I followed with intense interest. Otherwise I skipped many and studied the masters of theoretical physics with religious dedication at home.*[116]

In March 1899 he was officially reprimanded for poor attendance by Jean Pernet, Professor of Experimental Physics. Pernet was furious when he saw Einstein discard the instructions for an experiment without reading them, but when he complained to an assistant about Einstein, he was annoyed to be told 'his solutions are right and the methods he uses are always of great interest'.[117] In July of that year Einstein caused an explosion in the laboratory and needed stitches after injuring his hand *rather seriously*.[118] Pernet told him sternly: 'There is no lack of eagerness and goodwill in your work, but a lack of capability.' The learned professor thought Einstein was not equal to the rigours of physics and suggested he study medicine, law, or philology instead.[119]

Although Einstein took more mathematics courses in his first year than his fellow students, he soon decided the subject was not essential for his work in physics – a decision he later regretted. His mathematics professor, Hermann Minkowski (1864–1909) – who

'He is intensely observant: his glance fixes on some detail and lingers over something which other people do not even notice. His interest will be suddenly aroused by statements made by specialists on questions which one would have thought alien to his world, secrets of craftsmanship and details of engineering. Everything ingenious in the material sphere engages his attention. If you watch him handle some object, he seems to take possession of it. He does not touch things as though he wanted to push them away as people do when their thoughts are elsewhere; he follows the outline, and taps the surface; he tests their faculties. He has a taste for solid things such as steel structures; he likes to watch a thing in the making. He feels at home in a world of stable laws, in a reality ruled by unalterable material facts.' ANTONINA VALLENTIN on Einstein (1954)[120] went on to develop Einstein's special theory of relativity into the idea of four-dimensional space-time – described him as a 'lazy dog'.[121] Before his great work on the general theory of relativity, Einstein saw mathematics as playing a strictly limited role. *Physics is essentially an intuitive and concrete science,* he said. *Mathematics is only a means for expressing the laws that govern phenomena.*[122] In his *Autobiographical Notes*, Einstein wrote about his time at the Poly and mathematics:

Working with chemist R W Bunsen (1811–99), the physicist Gustav Robert Kirchhoff (1824–87) discovered that in the gaseous state each chemical substance emits its own characteristic spectrum. Using the technique of spectroscopy they discovered the elements caesium and rubidium.

I had excellent teachers (for example, Hurwitz, Minkowski), so that I should have been able to obtain a mathematical training in depth. I worked most of the time in the physical laboratory, however, fascinated by the direct contact with experience. The balance of the time I used, in the main, in order to study at home the works of Kirchhoff, Helmholtz, Hertz, etc. The fact that I neglected mathematics to a certain extent had its cause not merely in my stronger interest in the natural sciences than in mathematics but also in the following peculiar experience. I saw that mathematics was split up into numerous specialities, each of which could easily absorb the short lifetime granted to us. Consequently, I saw myself in the position of Buridan's ass, which was unable to decide upon any particular bundle of hay. Presumably this was because my intuition was not strong enough in the field of mathematics to differentiate clearly the fundamentally important, that which is really basic, from the rest of the more or less dispensable erudition. Also, my interest in the study of nature was no doubt stronger; and it was not clear to me as a young

German physicist and physiologist Hermann Ludwig Ferdinand von Helmholtz (1821–94) developed British physicist Thomas Young's theory of colour vision (the Young-Helmholtz theory), published in his *Physiological Optics* (1856). He also contributed to the development of thermodynamics.

German physicist Heinrich Rudolf Hertz (1857–94) was the first to produce and detect radio waves (1888). James Clerk Maxwell (1831–79) had predicted the existence of electromagnetic radiation over a wide range of frequencies, but until Hertz's discovery radio-frequency radiation was unknown.

Hermann Minkowski

student that access to a more profound knowledge of the basic principles of physics depends on the most intricate mathematical methods. This dawned upon me only gradually after years of independent scientific work.[123]

Minkowski was a notoriously poor lecturer. In contrast, Professor H F Weber – who had been so impressed by Einstein's initial application to the Poly – had a high reputation among the students. At first Einstein described Weber's lectures on theoretical physics as masterly, but he soon came to the opinion that Weber's view of physics was outdated. Impatient to learn the latest scientific thinking, Einstein saw Weber as symptomatic of the *dogmatic rigidity* that prevailed in physics at the time: *In the beginning (if there was such a thing), God created Newton's laws of motion together with the necessary masses and forces. This is all; everything beyond this follows from the development of appropriate mathematical methods by means of deduction.*[124]

Even as a student, Einstein knew that the mechanical world view

British physicist and mathematician Sir Isaac Newton (1642–1727) discovered the law of gravitation and supplied the three laws of motion. He also invented the calculus and in optics he recognised that white light is a mixture of coloured rays that can be separated by refraction. His major works are *Philosophiae naturalis principia mathematica* (1686–7) and *Optics* (1704).

Newtonian mechanics: Newton's three laws of motion are: (1) a body remains at rest or moves with constant velocity in a straight line unless acted upon by a force; (2) the acceleration (a) of a body is proportional to the force (f) causing it. The constant of proportionality is the mass (m) of the body, so $f=ma$; (3) the action of a force always produces a reaction in the body. The reaction is of equal magnitude but opposite in direction to the action.

of Isaac Newton needed to be revised to incorporate a *profounder understanding of relationships*.[125] Unlike Weber, Einstein was fascinated by the Scottish physicist James Clerk Maxwell's brilliant theory of electromagnetism. According to Maxwell, electricity, magnetism and light were different aspects of the same phenomenon. His idea that electromagnetic waves travelled at the speed of light was *like a revelation* to Einstein, providing him with a key element of the special theory of relativity.[126] Inspired by the work of the chemist and physicist Michael Faraday (1791–1867), Maxwell showed that *there are electromagnetic phenomena that by their very nature are detached from all ponderable matter – namely the waves in empty space that consist of electro-magnetic 'fields'*.[127] Maxwell's field equations describing the movement of these electromagnetic waves resulted in physicists introducing the idea of an ether that permeates space. It was this, they thought, that conveyed the electromagnetic phenomena of light and radio waves. This ether was the subject of Einstein's first scientific essay and electromagnetism still fired his imagination. Maxwell, who died the year Einstein was born, was never mentioned in Weber's lectures, which stopped in the 1850s with German physicist Hermann von Helmholtz and the science of thermodynamics: *At the close of our studies*, wrote Einstein, *we knew all the past of physics but nothing of its present and future*.[128] So Einstein supplemented his studies by reading cutting-edge physics – works by Ludwig Boltzmann (1844–1906), H A Lorentz (1853–1928), and Ernst Mach (1838–1916), whose challenge to the absolutes of time and space *exercised a profound influence* upon him.[129]

Mach's *scepticism and independence* appealed to Einstein.[130] They were qualities he possessed in abundance himself. An irritated Weber once told him: 'You're a very clever boy, Einstein, an extremely clever boy, but you have one great fault: you'll never let yourself be told anything.'[131] Indicative of this lack of respect was the way Einstein always addressed him as *Herr Weber* rather than *Herr Professor*.[132] Even as a child, Maja recalls, Einstein gained a reputation with his

SCEPTICISM AND INDEPENDENCE

music teacher for being 'impertinent'.[133] According to one biographer, Einstein's character prevented him from fitting into the world of physics: 'At once warm and distant, *sachlich* and abstract, mocking and serious, Einstein's temperament excluded the pretension, pomposity, and jealousy that often radiated from his physicist colleagues.'[134]

Respect for rank or authority did not come easily for Einstein and in an age obsessed with such formalities he soon created enemies. An antagonism grew up between Weber and Einstein that was to cause serious difficulties for the young man at the start of his career. Although Einstein started out with a keen interest in practical experimentation, no doubt fuelled by his family background in electrotechnology, he soon began to rely on the published results of experiments, using these as the springboard for bold theoretical speculations. Weber 'became increasingly dissatisfied with the unorthodox student who cut too many corners'.[135] At the end of his studies Einstein applied to be Weber's assistant but the professor turned him down flat. Einstein's three fellow graduates all became assistants at the Poly and he even suspected Weber was trying to sabotage his chances of a position elsewhere. When the professor died in 1912, Einstein coldly announced: *Weber's death is good for the Poly.*[136]

It was the independence and freedom offered by a scientific career that attracted Einstein as a pupil at Aarau. *I am truly a 'lone traveller',* he wrote in 1930, *and have never belonged to my country, my home, my friends, or even my immediate family, with my whole heart. In the face of all this, I have never lost a sense of distance and the need for solitude.*[137] The beginning of his scientific career was spent in total isolation from the physics community. Ironically, from the 1920s Einstein became once again a lone voice in physics, as he criticised the development of quantum theory. But such was the brilliance of his insights into the structure of the universe, that science could not ignore him for long.

The Battle of Dollie
1896–1903

In Zurich, Einstein fell in love with fellow physics student Mileva Marić. They married in 1903, but the full story of their troubled relationship was revealed only comparatively recently with the publication of their love letters. These offer a fascinating insight into Einstein's personal life as well as glimpses into his science. The majority of the letters are from Einstein, carefully preserved by Mileva. When she died in 1948 they passed to their son, Hans Albert. The executors of Einstein's estate, Otto Nathan and Helen Dukas, prevented their publication until 1987, 14 years after Hans Albert's death. The letters show that the couple had an illegitimate daughter, Lieserl, whom Einstein probably never saw and whose ultimate fate remains a mystery. His correspondence, which is gradually being published, has exposed a new and less flattering side to his character, revealing 'a man whose public words and private deeds were often at odds, and whose outward serenity concealed inner confusion'.[138] The great physicist, who jokingly referred to himself as a *Jewish saint*, was only human after all.[139]

Einstein with Mileva Marić

Before they met, Einstein and Mileva were linked by a river. The Danube flows east across Europe, from the Black Forest in Germany to Romania's coast on the Black

A NEW LOVE

Sea. It passes through Ulm, across southern Germany and into the lands of the former Austro-Hungarian Empire – through Vienna and down into the present-day Serbian cities of Novi Sad and Kać, where Mileva's father was born and which later became the Marić family home. Mileva was born on 19 December 1875 in the village of Titel, part of Vojvodina in what was then southern Hungary. Her father, Miloš, was a minor official in the Hungarian civil service. In 1867 he married Marija Ružić, the daughter of a prosperous land-owning family, and three years after Mileva's birth the family bought a large property in Kać.

Although her parents were Serbian, German was spoken at home and Mileva grew up fluent in the language. Something of a prodigy herself, she was granted special permission to study physics at the all-male Royal Gymnasium in Zagreb, which was almost unheard of in the days of the Austro-Hungarian Empire. In 1894 she lived up to her father's expectations by attaining the highest grades for both maths and physics. As women were not allowed to attend university, Mileva continued her studies in Switzerland, as did many women at this time. After a year at a girls' preparatory school in Zurich, Mileva was admitted to Zurich University to study medicine in spring 1896, then changed after a semester to physics at the Poly.

The first evidence of their relationship comes in a letter she wrote to Einstein in October 1897. She had broken off her studies to spend the winter semester in Heidelberg where she attended physics lectures by Philipp Lenard (1862–1947). Ironically, although Mileva enjoyed Lenard's lectures, he went on to become one of Einstein's most savage critics. Quite why Mileva interrupted her studies to stay in Heidelberg is unclear. It is possible she was already in love with Einstein and wanted time to think. He had written Mileva a four-page letter – unusual for a self-confessed *lazy* letter writer[140] – and she had already told her parents about him: 'Papa gave me some tobacco that I'm to give you personally. He's eager to whet your appetite for our little land of outlaws. I told him all about you – you absolutely must come back with me some day – the two of you would really have a lot to talk about!'[141] Einstein called Mileva a *little runaway*, and told her to *return as soon as possible*.[142] She followed his advice, starting her courses again in April 1898. Whatever the reason for her stay in Heidelberg, it meant she had to take her intermediate exams in October 1899, a year after Einstein.

From 1898, Mileva became Einstein's closest companion and confidante in his quest to revolutionise physics. *How closely our mental and physiological lives are linked*, he wrote to her in March 1899.[143] They studied together, shared lecture notes, and discussed the latest ideas in physics into the early hours. In September 1899 he told her he was reading Helmholtz, Boltzmann, and Mach, but he felt obliged to add: *I give you my solemn promise that I'll go over everything with you.*[144] Even in his love letters, science is never far from Einstein's thoughts. Terms of endearment share the same sentence with the great names of physics. In August 1899, while holidaying with his *mother hen* and sister, Einstein wrote that they seemed *petty and philistine*[145] and he longed for Mileva: *We understand one another's dark souls so well . . .*[146] As one of his biographers comments, although Einstein was 'well travelled for his years, [. . .] he had never come across anything as exotic as a woman physicist'.[147] His female company until now had been bourgeois and cultured. Although they could accompany him on the piano when he played the violin, they were incapable of following him intellectually. But Mileva was different and he fell deeply in love: *I'm so lucky to have found you, a creature who is my equal, and who is as strong and as independent as I am! I feel alone with everyone except you.*[148] Einstein thought he had found his ideal soulmate with whom he could lead a bohemian life of the mind.

Mileva lived at 50 Plattenstrasse, a boarding house popular among Balkan students. A fellow Serb who also lived there, Milana Bota, wrote to her mother describing Mileva: 'She seems to be a very good girl, and very smart and serious; small, delicate, brunette, ugly.'[149] Another student, Ida Kaufler, was rather more perceptive: 'She was very witty and knew how to make the whole group laugh irresistibly, while remaining serious herself. When she was pleased about something, a transient smile passed across her face. Her pleasure was joyful and infectious, and she was beautiful in those moments. Her eyes glowed with an inner fire. Her cheerfulness cast a shine on herself and everyone around her.'[150] Susanne, the daughter of Einstein's landlady, noticed that he often worked with Mileva and described her as a 'modest, unassuming creature'.[151] She remembered how Einstein once leapt to Mileva's defence: 'Referring one day to her limp, one of Einstein's colleagues said "I should never have the courage to marry a woman unless she were absolutely sound." Whereupon Einstein replied quite calmly: *But she has such a lovely voice*.'[152] Mileva's limp was due to a displaced left hip, a congenital condition common among Balkan women that also affected her younger sister, Zorka. But, as in his science, Einstein had a gift for seeing beyond the surface of things to the underlying beauty. He could never keep a

Einstein with Mileva

secret from his mother and already in March 1899 he had shown her Mileva's photograph, saying *Yes, yes, she certainly is a clever one.*[153]

Every evening, Einstein – who was living at nearby 4 Unionstrasse from November 1899 – would visit Mileva in her fourth-floor room to study together. Her friends were suspicious of this scruffy 'German'. (Milana told her mother that she and Mileva 'rarely get together because of that German of hers whom I hate'.)[154] In their letters, Einstein first addresses Mileva as *Esteemed Miss*, but soon starts to call her *LD*, short for *Liebes Doxerl*, a south German pet name meaning 'doll'. By the end of 1899 this had become *dear sweet Dollie* and she was addressing her letters to *dear Johnnie.*[155] Although they did not live together, Einstein was already referring to Mileva's room as *our household.*[156] According to Peter Michelmore, the first biographer to work closely with Einstein's elder son, Mileva was a practical woman with a strong character: 'She judged people quickly and was firm in her likes and dislikes. She had a definite viewpoint in any argument. She planned her studies and her routine well ahead. She tried to bring a sense of order into Albert's life, too. [. . .] She made him eat regularly and told him how to budget his allowance properly. Frequently, she was infuriated at his absent-mindedness. He would look at this angry little girl stamping her foot and a glint of devilment would come into his eyes. He would make a joke or pull a face and slowly charm her out of her mood.'[157] It is clear that Einstein enjoyed playing the role of the wayward child. Mileva reminded him of his mother, as a letter from Milan shows: *You came vividly to mind during a harsh scolding I just received.*[158] In another letter he writes *I'm beginning to feel the absence of your beneficent thumb, under which I'm always kept in line.*[159]

They both spent the summer holidays of 1899 studying, Mileva on her parents' rural estate in Kać, Einstein in Milan. Mileva was revising for her intermediate exams which Einstein had taken the previous year. He was preoccupied with scientific problems that would lead to major discoveries in six years time. Once again, the focus of his interest was electrodynamics, exploring the forces

Hermann Helmholtz

generated by electric and magnetic fields and trying to account for the behaviour of charged bodies in motion, such as electrons. In his letters from August and September 1899 we catch a glimpse of the ideas simmering in his mind. After reading Helmholtz and Hertz he comments: *I'm convinced more and more that the electrodynamics of moving bodies as it is presented today doesn't correspond to reality, and that it will be possible to present it in a simpler way. The introduction of the term 'ether' into theories of electricity has led to the conception of a medium whose motion can be described, without, I believe, being able to ascribe physical meaning to it. I think that electrical forces can be directly defined only for empty space.*[160] This significant statement shows how Einstein was beginning to grapple with themes central to his famous 1905 paper on relativity, in which he would dismiss the whole notion of the ether, an invisible substance that physicists assumed filled space and through which electromagnetic waves (radio, light, etc) flowed like waves in water.

Mileva passed her intermediate exams, but only just, coming fifth out of six candidates. In his exams the year before, Einstein had been top of his class. The following year, the first of a new century, they took their final exams. Together, Einstein and Mileva worked on heat conduction for their dissertations. For once the two of them stayed in Zurich for the spring holiday, writing up their research. Neither of them handed in an exceptional piece of work. Out of a maximum of 6 marks, Mileva got 4 and Einstein 4.5. They also performed worse than expected in their exams, with Einstein and Mileva finishing fourth and fifth respectively out of a group of five. When the results were announced on 28 July 1900, Einstein had passed, along with his friends Marcel Grossmann, Jakob Ehrat, and Louis Kollros. They were now qualified to teach mathematics and science in secondary schools. Mileva had failed. For the first time ever she had to return to her parents in August 1900 bearing bad news.

It was to be a difficult year. Einstein and Mileva wanted to marry, but first they had to ask their parents' permission. Mileva thought her family would not oppose a marriage, but Einstein's mother presented more of a problem. The first hint of trouble came when a mutual friend, Helene Kaufler, a history student at Zurich University who lived in Mileva's boarding house, visited Einstein's parents in the summer while holidaying at Lake Garda, Italy. Helene reported that Pauline Einstein had made fun of Mileva. It must have been a cruel blow to Mileva, who had been 'anxiously' waiting for news of Pauline's opinion of her. She wrote despairingly to Helene: 'Do you think that she does not like me at all? Did she make fun of me really badly?'[161]

Then, during his summer holiday at the Swiss resort of Melchtal, Einstein revealed the couple's plans with characteristic frankness. 'So, what will become of your Dollie now?' asked Mrs Einstein after he had told her the good news of his exam results. *My wife*, replied Einstein.[162] In a letter, Einstein tries to make light of what happened next, but its effect on Mileva is easy to imagine: *Mama threw herself on to the bed, buried her head in the pillow, and wept like a child. After regaining her composure she immediately shifted to a desperate attack: 'You are ruining your future and destroying your opportunities . . . No decent family will have her . . . If she gets pregnant you'll really be in a mess.'*[163] These last words were to prove prophetic and would haunt Einstein, but to his mother he denied they had been *living in sin*. However, the row continued that evening and Einstein dutifully reported his mother's criticisms to Mileva: *'Like you, she is a book – but you ought to have a wife'*, and *'By the time you're 30 she'll be an old witch.'*[164] When Einstein returned to Milan with his mother, her snide remarks about Mileva's age and intellectual interests were supplanted by unjustified fears that Mileva was not *healthy*.[165] Underlying his mother's attitude to Mileva was a widespread German prejudice against the Serbs and Slavs in general.

Einstein's summer holidays (from the end of July to October 1900) dragged by very slowly. There were frequent arguments and he commented wryly that now he knew there were worse things in life than exams. But, he wrote, *the valiant Swabian is not afraid* and he was convinced he would win *the battle of Dollie*.[166] He boasted that his parents had *less stubbornness in their entire bodies than I have in my little finger*.[167] Mileva's parents were less hostile to the match and Einstein was pleased they had not grown *stale* like his own *philistine* parents: *Your parents are proof that people don't have to wind up this way – they must be wonderful. But don't tell them too much about me or they might get frightened. I would have been smarter to have kept my mouth shut*.[168] He looked forward to the time when he and Mileva would be reunited in Zurich, studying and drinking coffee: *I can't wait until I have you again, my everything, my little so-and-so, my street urchin, my little rascal!*[169] He told her proudly how he had now learnt to shave himself rather than going to the barber: *You'll see, Dollie! I can always do it while you're making coffee for lunch, so that I don't pound the books as usual while poor Dollie has to cook, and while lazy Johnnie lolls about after hastily obeying the rapidly uttered command: 'grind this'.*[170] It seems the division of labour in their *household* was already a bone of contention, even before they were officially living together. Whether or not Mileva was happy to be cast in the role of 'Hausfrau', Einstein approved of her *henlike enthusiasm* – he even sent her a drawing of his *gigantic little foot* so that she could knit him some socks![171]

Added to the couple's worries about their marriage was the no less urgent need for Einstein to find a job. He had hoped to become an assistant at the Poly, but neither Pernet nor Weber was interested. Instead he had to look for teaching work while beginning his doctoral thesis under Weber's critical eye. Mileva, too, hoped to work on a doctoral dissertation and to retake her final exams. When Einstein returned to Zurich in the autumn he earned some money teaching for eight hours a week and doing calculations for Alfred

Wolfer (1854–1931) at the Swiss Federal Observatory. It was a precarious existence, as he told Helene Kaufler in October: *My Dollie arrived here yesterday together with her sister, so that I hang out at her place all day long, as always. Neither of us has a job and we support ourselves by private lessons – when we can pick up some, which is still very questionable. Is this not a journeyman's or even a gypsy's life? But I believe that we'll remain cheerful in it as ever.*[172]

Mileva was less positive: 'When are we going to reach the point at which we'll be allowed to acknowledge our love before the whole world,' she wrote to Helene, 'it

Oh my! That Johnnie boy!
So crazy with desire,
While thinking of his Dollie,
His pillow catches fire.

When my sweetie mopes around the house
I shrivel up so small,
But she only shrugs her shoulders
And doesn't care at all.

To my folks all this
Does seem a stupid thing,
But they never say a single word
For fear of Albert's sting!

My little Dollie's little beak,
It sings so sweet and fine;
And afterwards I cheerfully
Close its song with mine.

EINSTEIN to Mileva, 20 August 1900[173]

almost seems to me that I'll not live long enough to see it.'[174] In another letter, she spoke darkly of the 'slanders and intrigues' she had suffered in her relationship with Einstein, but adds 'I am happy that he loves me so much, and what else do I need?'[175]

There was one ray of hope. In December 1900 Einstein had his first scientific paper accepted for publication: 'You can imagine how proud I am of my darling,' wrote Mileva. 'This is not just an everyday paper, but a very significant one, it deals with the theory of liquids.'[176] Einstein's account of molecular forces in capillary action appeared in the prestigious German physics journal *Annalen der Physik* in March 1901. Einstein continued working on this idea throughout that year, hoping to develop it into a doctoral thesis. Although he later described this and another paper on the same theme as *worthless*, it gave the couple hope that Einstein would soon find an academic position.[177]

Throughout the spring of 1901 Einstein tried desperately to find a position as an assistant, the first rung on the academic ladder. *I will have soon graced all the physicists from the North Sea to the Southern tip of Italy with my offer,* he wrote on 4 April.[178] The bleakness of their situation – he without a job and she with no teaching qualification – is apparent in Mileva's letters to Helene: 'The truth is, we haven't yet the slightest idea what fate has in store for us.'[179] At the end of the year she gave two reasons why Einstein was still unsuccessful: 'my sweetheart has a very wicked tongue and is a Jew into the bargain.'[180] Unknown to Einstein, his worried father even wrote to the great chemist Wilhelm Ostwald (1853–1932) asking if he could help his son. Ostwald did not reply, but ten years later he would nominate Einstein for a Nobel Prize.

On 13 April 1901, the same day that his father wrote to Ostwald, Einstein received a letter from his friend Marcel Grossmann confirming that he was in line for a full-time position at the Swiss Patent Office in Bern. Grossmann's father, a friend of the director of the patent office, had recommended Einstein personally. The following day – as he told Mileva in an excited letter – Einstein received a letter offering him two months teaching mathematics at a technical school in the town of Winterthur. *Isn't this almost too much at once?* he wrote, saying of the position at the patent office: *Imagine what a wonderful job this would be for me! I'll be mad with joy if something should become of that!*[181] At last it looked as though fortune was smiling on the couple.

Just before he was due to begin teaching in May, Einstein and Mileva met at Lake Como for a brief holiday together, he travelling from Milan, she from Zurich. He had to work hard to convince her to meet him: *You absolutely must come to see me in Como, you sweet little witch,* he wrote. *You'll see for yourself how bright and cheerful I've become and how all my frowning has been forgotten.*[182] Once he is employed at the patent office he promises to appoint her as his *dear little scientist.* As an after-thought he adds: *come to me in Como and bring my blue nightshirt so we can wrap ourselves up in it.*[183]

Later Mileva told Helene the trip 'was so beautiful that it made me forget all my sorrows'.[184] They walked around the town of Como before taking a boat ride to the Villa Carlotti, famed for its azalea gardens which were in full bloom. It is not known where they stayed, but they travelled back to Switzerland through the picturesque Splügen Pass on the border between Switzerland and Italy. They made the journey on a horse-drawn sleigh, huddled under furs to protect them from the biting cold: 'The Splügen, which we wanted to cross, lay deep in snow, which in some spots reached a height of 6 m[eters],' reported Mileva. 'Therefore we rented a very small sledge [. . .] which has just enough room for two people in love with each other, and the coachman stands on a little plank at the rear and prattles all the time and calls you "signora" – could you think of anything more beautiful?'[185] At Como Einstein and Mileva reaffirmed their love for each other and looked forward to a time when they could live together as husband and wife.

Afterwards Einstein travelled to Winterthur, an industrial city set in rolling countryside, 25km north-east of Zurich where his two months of teaching passed without incident. He lived at 38 Schaffhauserstrasse. Most Sundays he would make the half-hour train journey to Zurich to see Mileva, who once asked her landlady if Einstein might stay overnight in one of the empty rooms in the house. In a letter she told him: 'My God, how beautiful the world will look when I'm your little wife, you'll see. There will be no happier woman in the whole world.'[186] It was on one of these weekend visits that Mileva revealed she was pregnant. In a letter from late May, Einstein wrote: *Be happy and don't fret, darling. I won't leave you and will bring everything to a happy conclusion. You just have to be patient! You'll see that my arms aren't so bad to rest in, even if things are beginning a little awkwardly. How are you, darling? How's the boy?*[187]

As well as reassuring her, Einstein still found time to discuss his scientific ideas. He had written to the renowned physicist Paul Drude (1863–1906), taking him to task for what he considered to be errors in his electron theory. But if fatherhood did not worry Einstein,

A HAPPY CONCLUSION

Mileva knew all too well the impact it would have on her own studies. Not only was she working on her doctoral dissertation but she had to re-sit her final exams in July. At Lake Como Einstein had convinced her that marriage was just around the corner. Now things looked more uncertain than ever. The stigma of an illegitimate child would damage their future prospects in society. Maja was already saying that according to the Wintelers Einstein had been *leading a life of debauchery in Zurich*.[188] True to form, Einstein buried his head in his books and chose to stay in Winterthur after his contract ended to continue working on his doctoral thesis.

All alone, Mileva became increasingly depressed. She pleaded with Einstein to visit her parents in the summer: 'It would make me so happy! [. . .] And when my parents see the two of us together in front of them all their doubts will disappear.'[189] But instead Einstein joined his mother on holiday in Mettmenstetten. He reported that things were less stormy now and wished Mileva luck in her exams. By 26 July she knew the worst: she had failed again. Her chances of becoming a teacher were as far off as ever. Depressed, Mileva prepared for the long journey home. It would not be an easy homecoming: she had to tell her parents not only about her poor results but also that she was pregnant. In the deeply conservative and rural region where she had grown up, this would bring nothing but shame on her family. As Einstein would not come with her, she asked him to explain to her father his intention to marry her. 'Just write a short letter to my Papa; by and by I'll give him the necessary information, the unpleasant news as well,' she told Einstein, adding: 'Will you send me the letter so I can see what you've written?'[190] It is clear she did not trust him to say the right thing. While Mileva broke the news to her parents, Einstein continued working on his doctoral thesis and looking for teaching posts. Eventually he found one in nearby Schaffhausen, tutoring an English boy, Louis Cahen, who intended to study architecture at the Poly.

In October Mileva made the two-day train journey from Novi Sad to Zurich. At first she stayed with Milana, who wrote to her mother that Mileva had 'passed her doctorate and is searching for a position in Zagreb'.[191] Pregnant and unmarried, she had no hope of becoming a teacher, but Mileva kept her pregnancy so secret that even Helene did not know. These were 'awful times' for Mileva.[192] To make matters worse, Einstein's parents wrote a letter to her father and mother 'in which they reviled me to such an extent that it was a disgrace'.[193] The letter caused a storm in the Marić household and 'much suffering' to Mileva. 'I wouldn't have thought it possible that there could exist such heartless and outright wicked people,' she wrote bitterly to Helene.[194] Upset, she wanted to be near Einstein in Schaffhausen. Aware that her 'funny figure' might cause a scandal, she went to a hotel in nearby Stein am Rhein, a beautiful medieval village in Switzerland.[195] Her two surviving letters make for sad reading. She longs to be with Einstein and asks why he cannot make the short trip to see her. Instead he sent her some books to read. It is not known if Einstein ever visited her. She left on 14 November, catching an early morning train for Zurich. They could have met briefly on the platform at Schaffhausen, where her train paused for half an hour before continuing to its destination. From Zurich Mileva caught the first of three trains that would take her back to Novi Sad.

Her parents had resigned themselves to the situation. With some relief, Einstein wrote that he was glad they had *calmed down and now trust me more*.[196] He was even able to make a joke about it. Tell your mother, he wrote to Mileva, that *I'm looking forward to the spanking with which she will do me honour some day*.[197] By December they had chosen names for the child, Mileva preferring to think of it as a girl called Lieserl and he a boy called Hanserl. Einstein was in buoyant mood, certain that he would get the patent office job in Bern – by spring 1902, he predicted, they would be the *happiest people on earth*, free to continue their bohemian life together: *We'll be students (horribile dictu) as long as we live and won't give a damn about the world*.[198]

But a cloud remained on the horizon, and even Einstein with his talent for burying his head in the sand could not ignore it: *The only problem that still needs to be resolved*, he wrote to Mileva, *is how to keep our Lieserl with us; I wouldn't want to have to give her up. Ask your Papa; he's an experienced man, and knows the world better than your overworked, impractical Johnnie.*[199] However, in one of Mileva's letters she mentions Helene and tells Einstein 'we must treat her well because she can help us with something important . . .'[200] It seems likely that Mileva planned to ask the now-married Helene to adopt their child.

On 18 December Einstein formally applied for the position of Engineer Class II at the Federal Office for Intellectual Property in Bern. The next day, assured of success, he wrote to Mileva that he was *absolutely crazy with happiness.*[201] He had also talked to Professor Kleiner in Zurich about his doctoral dissertation on the kinetic theory of gases. The professor had been impressed enough to offer Einstein an academic reference. The future looked rosy. They would be *rich* he boasted to Mileva. The salary was from 3,500 to 4,500 francs and, although a friend doubted you could *get by on 4,000 with a wife*, Einstein felt certain he could.[202] *When you're my dear little wife we'll diligently work on science together so we don't become old philistines, right?*[203] He was so confident about the future that at the end of January 1902 he resigned from his position at Schaffhausen and moved to Bern.

In February he received a letter from Mileva's father. *I was frightened out of my wits when your father's letter came*, wrote Einstein on 4 February 1902, *because I had already sensed something wrong.*[204] Mileva had given birth to a girl. Very little is known about Lieserl. She was probably born on 27 January. The letter from Miloš Marić has been lost or destroyed, but it is clear from Einstein's worried reply that the birth was difficult. A breech delivery is five times more likely for a woman with Mileva's congenital hip displacement. There are no records of Lieserl being christened, but it is likely that a Serbian Orthodox ceremony was conducted in private. Like any new father, Einstein was full of questions about his newborn daughter: *Is she healthy, and does she cry properly? What are her eyes like? Which one of us does she more resemble? Who is giving her milk? Is she hungry? She must be completely bald. I love her so much and don't even know her yet! Couldn't you have a photograph made of her when you've regained your health? Is she looking at things yet? Now you can make observations. I'd like to make a Lieserl myself sometime – it must be fascinating! She's certainly able to cry already, but won't know how to laugh until much later. Therein lies a profound truth. When you feel a little better you'll have to draw a picture of her!*[205]

The two remaining letters in the Einstein archive from February 1902 are missing their final pages and contain no mention of Lieserl. The only other reference to their daughter in the surviving letters occurs more than a year and a half later, in September 1903. Writing to Mileva, who was visiting her parents and Lieserl, Einstein says: *I'm very sorry about what has befallen Lieserl. It's so easy to suffer lasting effects from scarlet fever. If only this will pass. As what is the child registered? We must take precautions that problems don't arise for her later.*[206] These cryptic comments have caused much speculation. Mileva had probably returned to arrange for their daughter's adoption, possibly by Helene in Belgrade. This would explain Einstein's concern about future problems, suggesting the need to conceal her true identity. But the mention of scarlet fever also raises the possibility that Lieserl suffered medical complications from this serious disease or even died. According to Swiss law, when Einstein finally married Mileva their daughter automatically became legitimate. It is unclear, therefore, why he was unwilling to bring Lieserl to Bern. It has been suggested that Lieserl was mentally handicapped, but the evidence is sketchy.[207] Possibly her parents were too afraid of offending Swiss propriety, although Einstein usually despised such *philistine* considerations.

The fate of Einstein's daughter remains a mystery. Many documents are missing; some, such as those in the possession of Helene, were deliberately destroyed, perhaps to protect the new identity of the child. Whatever happened, most people agree that Mileva was a changed woman by the time she returned to Bern in September 1903.

49

Five Papers that Changed the World
1902–1905

Einstein arrived in Bern in February 1902. Initially he lived in the old town at 32 Gerechtigkeitsgasse, a cobbled street that had changed little in 500 years. *It's wonderful here in Bern,* he wrote to Mileva. *An ancient, thoroughly pleasant city in which one can live exactly as in Zurich. There are very old arcades stretching along both sides of the streets, so you can walk from one end of the city to the other in the worst rain without getting noticeably wet.*[208] He included a diagram of his first-floor room: *I have a large, pleasant room with a very comfortable sofa. It only costs 23 francs. That's not too much. I also have six upholstered chairs and three cabinets; you could hold a meeting in this place.*[209] However, when his friend Max Talmud paid an unexpected visit he did not share Einstein's enthusiasm, describing it as a 'small, poorly furnished room'.[210]

The city of Bern on the River Aare

He was shocked by Einstein's 'great poverty'. It had been rash of him to arrive in Bern before receiving a definite job offer from the patent office. Einstein had no allowance and the little he had saved from teaching would not last long. One of the first things he did, therefore, was place an advertisement in the newspaper offering private lessons in maths and physics. The man who would soon be hailed as the greatest physicist since Isaac Newton even offered free trial lessons. Einstein's advertisement appeared in the same week in which he learnt he was a father.

From a financial point of view, marriage was still out of the question. He quipped that he could make more money busking with his violin than from teaching. Furthermore, Pauline Einstein was still stubbornly opposed to his marrying Mileva. Unaware that she was a grandmother, she wrote to Einstein's *Mamma No 2*,[211] Pauline Winteler, stating her strong opposition to 'the liaison of Albert and Miss Marić'. 'We don't want ever to have anything to do with her,' she wrote. 'This Miss Marić is causing me the bitterest hours of my life, if it were in my power, I would make every possible effort to banish her from our horizon, I really dislike her.'[212] Einstein's mother had not even met Mileva, but she was convinced the Wintelers would make more suitable in-laws than some obscure Serbian family. Unsurprisingly, one of the reasons Einstein enjoyed life in Bern was the absence of any *philistine acquaintances.*[213]

He ignored his mother's objections and pinned his hopes on becoming a patent officer. In the meantime he reassured Mileva that his private tutoring was going well. One of his first students was Maurice Solovine who had come to Bern from Romania to study philosophy and wanted to be initiated into the wonders of physics. On first meeting Einstein, Solovine was 'struck by the extraordinary brilliance of his large eyes'.[214] They talked for two hours, continuing their discussion of physics and philosophy in the cobbled street outside. After a few lessons they became firm friends and remained in touch until Einstein's death.

Although he was poor, friendship mattered more to Einstein than money and Solovine's payments were soon forgotten. Conrad Habicht, whom Einstein had met in Schaffhausen and was now working on a doctorate in mathematics, joined their regular discussions, usually over a frugal meal of 'sausage, a piece of Gruyère cheese, fruit, a small jar of honey and one or two cups of tea'.[215] Together they worked their way through an impressive reading list of scientific, philosophical, and even literary works, including *The*

Grammar of Science (1892) by biologist Karl Pearson (1857–1936), *A System of Logic* (1843) by John Stuart Mill (1806–73), *A Treatise of Human Nature* (1739) by Scottish philosopher David Hume (1711–76), the dialogues of Plato (*c.*427–347BC), as well as works by German philosopher Gottfried Wilhelm Leibniz (1646–1716), his contemporary Benedict de Spinoza (1632–77), and the novelist Charles Dickens (1812–70). This regular gathering of minds required a suitably portentous name and with more than a touch of irony they christened themselves the Olympia Academy. Recalling these bohemian days, with little or no money but plenty of free-wheeling philosophical debates, Solovine said 'What a beautiful thing joyous poverty is!'[216] Later Einstein wrote about their *wonderful* times in Bern, noting that *our Academy was less childish than those respectable ones that I later got to know.*[217]

Isolated as he was from the scientific community, the Olympia Academy provided Einstein with an essential intellectual stimulus and the works they read together helped shape his approach to science. He disagreed with Mill's praise of the inductive method in science: *There is no inductive method which could lead to the fundamental concepts of physics,* he wrote. *Failure to understand this fact constituted the basic philosophical error of so many investigators of the nineteenth century.*[218] Einstein's approach was deductive. He assumed certain truths about the physical world from which he deduced consequences that could be measured against observations and experiments. Most scientists worked the other way round, starting from experimental data and developing a theory to explain the evidence. It was the 18th-century philosopher David Hume that Einstein credited with giving him the confidence to work in this unusual way: *Hume saw clearly that certain concepts, as for example that of causality, cannot be deduced from the material of experience by logical methods.*[219]

The Austrian physicist and philosopher Ernst Mach's scepticism towards the concepts of mechanics also proved influential. Mach famously claimed that Newton's absolute space was a 'conceptual monstrosity' and time was no more than a convenient metaphysical term.[220] Likewise in *Science and Hypothesis* (1902) the French mathematician Henri Poincaré (1854–1912) questioned the absolutes of space, time, and even our sense of simultaneity: 'There is no absolute time. When we say that two periods are equal, the statement has no meaning and can only acquire a meaning by a convention.'[221] Such ideas were crucial to Einstein's thinking. Solovine remembered how *Science and Hypothesis* 'profoundly impressed us and held us spellbound for weeks on end'.[222] Indeed, in 1904 Poincaré presented a paper in America in which he proposed a new theory of mechanics and a principle of relativity in which 'no velocity could surpass that of light'.[223] Impressed though they were by the Frenchman's ideas, Poincaré and physicists like H A Lorentz were still working inductively, piecing together experimental evidence to create a theory. But the facts simply did not add up and, close though they were, it was Einstein who resolved the problems in his 1905 theory of relativity. One of the main sticking points at the time was the problematic notion of an all-pervading ether. By adopting a deductive approach, Einstein was able to discard this and revolutionise physics.

At the end of May 1902, Einstein was finally interviewed by Friedrich Haller, the director of the patent office. Haller was impressed and Einstein began work on the 23rd as a Technical Expert Third Class. The worst of Einstein's money troubles were at an end. However, there were other matters to worry about. After his initial excited letters to Mileva in February there is a gap in their correspondence which, as one biographer has said, conveniently conceals their 'agonizing over Lieserl'.[224] Einstein had moved to 43a Thunstrasse at the beginning of June. The day before, Mileva had moved into a room on the same street at number 24. Lieserl was six months old, but Mileva had left her behind to be with Einstein. No longer entitled to a student visa, she could stay in Bern for only two months at a time. It was a difficult period for them both. After one argument, Einstein wrote a note telling Mileva that he thought about her *with*

THE TECHNICAL EXPERT

witnesses were Einstein's friends Solovine and Habicht. The couple could not afford a honeymoon so they spent the evening celebrating modestly with friends. Neither the bride nor the groom's family was present. When Einstein and his bride arrived at his lodgings in Archivstrasse that night he found as usual that he had forgotten his keys and had to rouse the landlord.

Towards the end of his life Einstein claimed that he had married merely out of a *sense of duty*.[228] But in 1903, writing from their new apartment at 18 Tillierstrasse, he said he was *living a very pleasant, cosy life with my wife. She takes excellent care of everything, cooks well, and is always cheerful*.[229] He was also enjoying his work at the patent office: *it is uncommonly diversified and there is much thinking to be done*, he said.[230] Mileva told a different story, however, saying Einstein had 'eight hours a day of very boring work' and that he was thinking of turning to teaching again.[231]

The secret they shared undoubtedly cast a shadow over their lives, and some of their friends described Mileva as 'gloomy, laconic and distrustful'.[232] The reason for this is clearer today. In autumn 1903 they reached a decision about Lieserl. They were now both Swiss citizens, but for some reason they decided not to bring her to Bern. Mileva travelled to her homeland in late August 1903, stopping on the way to write Einstein a touching postcard: 'Dear Johnnie, I'm already in Budapest. It's going quickly, but badly. I'm not feeling well at all. What are you up to, little Johnnie? Write me soon, okay? Your poor Dollie.'[233] Mileva's sickness on the journey was possibly due to the fact she was pregnant again, for in September Einstein wrote: *I'm not the least bit angry that poor Dollie is hatching a new chick*. The child would be *a new Lieserl*, he wrote, a phrase that implies the 'old' Lieserl was to have no further place in their lives.[234]

The *new chick* was Hans Albert, born 14 May 1904. They had moved in October the previous year to 49 Kramgasse (now an Einstein museum), a modest second-floor apartment just up the road from the room he had first rented in Bern.

HANS ALBERT IS BORN

Einstein with Mileva and their son Hans Albert in Bern, 1904

Married and with a regular income, Einstein began what were to become the most productive and creative years of his life. In spring 1904 he had his fifth publication in the *Annalen*. His first two papers had focused on his search for a universal molecular force and are, according to physicist and Einstein biographer Abraham Pais, 'justly forgotten'.[235] However, Einstein's 1904 paper 'On the General Molecular Theory of Heat' was the latest of a series of three papers on statistical physics, using the atomic theory of gases to establish the foundations of thermodynamics. Writing to his friend Habicht in April 1904, Einstein had announced two pieces of news almost in the same breath: *We are expecting a baby in a few weeks. I have now found the relationship between the magnitude of the elementary quanta of matter and the wavelengths of radiation in an exceedingly simple way.*[236] It marked the beginning of his attempt to explore the significance of German physicist Max Planck's ground-breaking work on black-body radiation. In 1900, Planck had explained this using a model in which energy was produced in discrete bundles, or pulses, which he termed 'quanta'. This went against the contemporary understanding of electromagnetic phenomena, such as light, which was viewed as a continuous wave. For this reason Planck himself doubted the reality of quanta, but for Einstein it revealed the weakness of current theories: *soon after 1900*, he wrote, *i.e., shortly after Planck's trailblazing work, it became clear to me that neither mechanics nor thermodynamics could* [. . .] *claim exact validity.*[237] His fascination with this problem led directly to a revolutionary paper he would write the following year, one that would eventually win him the Nobel Prize.

From summer 1904 to spring 1905 Habicht received a steady stream of petulant notes from Einstein summoning him to meetings of the Olympia Academy. *This is to beseech, warn, and order you to attend some of the academic sessions of our estimable academy*, commanded the physicist, berating his friend for his poor attendance record.[238]

Max Planck (1858–1947) studied physics in Berlin, writing his thesis on the second law of thermodynamics in 1879. At the end of the 1890s he began working on black-body or cavity radiation, an area of physics that had arisen out of the need to explain the relationship between the temperature of heated bodies (such as coal or metal) and the colour of the light they emitted. In 1900 this resulted in Planck's law predicting the intensity of black-body radiation. For the first time the notion of an energy quantum was introduced to physics, expressed by Planck's now famous equation: $E=hf$. It was an idea that would eventually raise the possibility of a fundamental divide between events at the atomic level and those in the everyday world.

Planck's work influenced Einstein's 1905 paper on the photoelectric effect. But, like Einstein, Planck could not accept the acausality inherent in quantum mechanics as it later developed.

Einstein's mind was buzzing with new ideas and he needed the intellectual stimulation of his friends more than ever. As far as the scientific community was concerned Einstein was an outsider: with no doctorate and a mere teaching diploma to his name, he had been unable to gain even the humblest academic position and did not have access to an academic library. For this reason he was always trying to *smuggle* his friends in *among the patent slaves*,[239] praising the patent office as a *secular monastery*[240] where he hoped to create his own alternative community of like-minded physicists and mathematicians.

One friend whom he did manage to entice into the Bern Patent Office was Michele Besso. Einstein respected Besso's wide knowledge of physics and philosophy as well as his friend's *extraordinarily keen mind*.[241] On Einstein's recommendation, Besso (who was six years older than Einstein) was appointed in summer 1904 as Technical Expert Second Class, a higher position than Einstein's. However, Einstein's generosity was rewarded in September when his position was made permanent and his salary increased, although it was still less than Besso's. But Einstein was never one to worry about *philistine* matters such as rank or salary. His real reward came from having someone to whom he could talk about physics.

Many years later he said of Besso: *I could not have found a better sounding-board in the whole of Europe*.[242] They used to walk home together from the patent office and their conversations provided a vital opportunity for Einstein to test out his startling ideas: 'The main subject of discussion was the discovery of light quanta. In endless conversations his cultured friend, in the role of critical disbeliever, defended Newton's recognized time and space concepts, into which he wove Mach's sensualistic positivism, and his analytical criticism of Newtonian mechanics.'[243] Throughout the second half of 1904 and into 1905, Einstein and Besso were often to be seen deep in conversation walking beside the fast-flowing River Aare or sitting in the Olympia Academy's favourite haunt, the Café Bollwerk. Although he never drank alcohol at these meetings, Einstein would always have *diffusion and the viscosity of dilute solutions of neutral substances. The third proves that, on the assumption of the molecular theory of heat, bodies on the order of magnitude 1/1000mm, suspended in liquids, must already perform an observable random motion that is produced by thermal motion; in fact, physiologists have observed 'unexplained' motions of suspended small, inanimate, bodies, which motions they designate as 'Brownian molecular motion'. The fourth paper is only a rough draft at this point, and is an electrodynamics of moving bodies which employs a modification of the theory of space and time.*[245]

The *very revolutionary* paper was completed first, on 17 March 1905 and published in the *Annalen* on 9 June. This paper, 'On a Heuristic Point of View Concerning the Production and Transformation of Light', attempts to resolve the problem of black-body radiation. In 1900, Planck had found a way to accurately predict the colour of glowing bodies, such as a red-hot poker, using an absolute constant (h) now known as Planck's constant, the value denoting each quantum increase in energy. According to Planck, energy could only be produced in certain fixed amounts or quanta. He later admitted that he introduced the quantum as an 'act of desperation'.[246] It made sense mathematically and worked in the laboratory, but it did not conform with any known physical principles. Indeed, physicists soon realised its implications were profound and challenged the whole structure of Newton's mechanical model of nature. Why was a vibrating atom in a heated body apparently only able to emit or absorb energy in quanta? Scientists could not understand why there was not a continuous rise or fall of energy, as in other physical systems.

Einstein approached this problem through another anomaly in physics – the photoelectric effect. This phenomenon had been noticed by Heinrich Hertz in 1888 while investigating the propagation of electromagnetic waves, research that led to the discovery of radio waves. If a piece of metal, such as zinc, is charged with static electricity (i.e. given a surplus of electrons) it will discharge or emit electrons when exposed to light. It is an effect that has since been put to many practical uses, being used in light sensors to control street lighting and also in television cameras. According to Maxwell, the colour of the light – corresponding in electromagnetic theory to the frequency of the wave – should make no difference to the emission of electrons. But it did. Red light had no effect, but purple (ultra-violet) light caused electrons to flow easily.

Einstein used Planck's notion of energy quanta to explain what was happening. As in his later paper on relativity, he realised that light was the key. In a truly revolutionary step that overturned 200 years of science, Einstein proposed that light was not a wave but was made up of particles of energy or quanta. Using Planck's constant, he suggested that the frequency (or colour) of the wave of light was a measure of the energy of its light particles, later called photons. Red light had a low frequency, therefore its particles lacked the energy required to knock electrons off the piece of metal. Ultra-violet light, however, with its high frequency, had no such problem and therefore was the most effective.

At the beginning of his paper Einstein pointed out that physicists had conflicting views. Planck described energy in terms of the quantum, whereas Maxwell saw energy and radiation, such as light, as a wave spreading out continuously through space. This contra-diction offended Einstein's belief in the underlying unity of nature. Since Thomas Young's landmark double-slit experiments with light at the start of the 19th century, scientists had accepted light was a wave. In the 1890s Hertz proudly proclaimed that 'the wave theory of light is from the point of view of human beings a certainty.'[247] But now Einstein attempted to resolve this contradiction by claiming that, at least in the photoelectric effect, light consisted not of waves but particles. His *light quantum hypothesis* argued that *when a light ray spreads out from a point source, the energy is not distributed continuously over an ever-increasing volume but consists of a finite number of energy quanta that are localized at points in space, move without dividing, and can be absorbed or generated only as complete units.*[248]

In 1910 Walther Nernst (1864–1941), professor of chemistry at

British scientist Thomas Young (1773–1829) is chiefly remembered for discovering the idea of interference in light waves in 1801. His famous double-slit experiment showed that light projected through two narrow slits on to a screen produces not the expected two stripes of light, one from each slit, but a complex pattern of light and shade known as an interference pattern. This experiment helped overturn the widely held view that light was a stream of bullet-like particles moving in a straight line.

Berlin, visited Einstein to discuss his intriguing quantum hypothesis. Later Nernst wrote: 'Einstein's quantum hypothesis is probably the strangest thing ever thought up. If correct, it opens entirely new roads both for so-called ether physics and for all molecular theories. If false, it will remain "a beautiful memory" for all times.' [249] But, as is often the case in science, resolving one problem merely creates another. Einstein's *light quantum hypothesis* argued that light consisted of particles. Yet in his paper on relativity, rather than contradicting Maxwell's notion of light as an electromagnetic wave, Einstein adopted a central part of Maxwell's theory by accepting a constant speed for light. This raised the question of how it was possible for light to be made up both of waves and particles, a paradox that was to occupy the quantum theorists for many years to come.

Einstein's next two papers, though not as revolutionary as the previous one, were every bit as influential. Indeed, at the centenary of Einstein's birth in 1979 it was calculated that these two were still among the top ten most cited papers published before 1912 in any exact science. Both of them were part of Einstein's attempt *to find facts that would guarantee as much as possible the existence of atoms of definite size.* [250] 'A New Determination of Molecular Dimensions' was the only one of Einstein's famous 1905 papers not to be published first in the prestigious *Annalen*. Instead, he used it as his third attempt to gain a doctorate, a process he had previously dismissed as a tedious *comedy*.[251] It was a case of third time lucky. Although the thesis was initially rejected by Professor Kleiner of Zurich University as too short, Einstein added an extra sentence and it was promptly accepted. The mathematical examiner even praised Einstein's 'fundamental mastery' of the maths, thereby overlooking a significant error in the calculations.[252] Although such influential scientists as Ostwald and Mach still doubted the reality of atoms, Einstein used the example of sugar dissolved in water to calculate the actual size of the sugar molecules – about one ten-millionth of a centimetre in radius, which was not far off. It was the simplicity of his model – assuming that the sugar molecules were small hard spheres and establishing a relationship between the volume of dissolved molecules and the increase in the viscosity of the solution – that was the key to the success of his theory.

Within days of completing this paper on 30 April, Einstein had also finished the next one, 'On the Motion of Small Particles Suspended in Liquids at Rest Required by the Molecular-Kinetic Theory of Heat'. According to Maja, when her brother was smoking his pipe or cigar he 'loved to observe the smoke clouds' wonderful shapes, and to study the motions of the individual particles of smoke and the relationships among them'.[253] It was just such a random motion of particles that Einstein sought to understand in this paper. Like the previous one it provided further powerful evidence for the existence of atoms and the possibility of an *exact determination of actual atomic sizes*.[254] In the 19th century, Scottish botanist Robert Brown (1773–1858) observed an erratic, zigzag motion in grains of pollen suspended in water that seemed to have nothing to do with currents. After he had eliminated the possibility that the pollen was alive, he observed the same phenomenon with other microscopic particles. Brownian motion, as it came to be called, can also be observed in particles suspended in air, smoke for instance. By the end of the 19th century it had been suggested that it could be explained by collisions between the particles and molecules.

Building on the ideas developed in his thesis, Einstein predicted that *bodies of a microscopically visible size suspended in liquids must, as a result of thermal molecular motions, perform motions of such magnitude that they can easily be observed with a microscope.*[255] He not only argued in his paper that suspended particles are constantly being bombarded by molecules, thus causing their random motion, but more importantly he provided the equations to predict the nature of this motion and the distance travelled by a particle. His ground-breaking use of statistical mechanics in this paper has proved influential across a wide range of disciplines, helping predict the dispersal of aerosols in the atmosphere and even the erratic movements of commodity markets.[256]

Innovative though these papers were, it is because of his work on the principle of relativity that Einstein's name has become synonymous with genius among non-scientists. The fourth paper that he mentions in his letter to Habicht was titled 'On the Electrodynamics of Moving Bodies' and was completed at the end of June 1905. The first sentence reads: *It is well known that Maxwell's electrodynamics – as usually understood at present – when applied to moving bodies, leads to asymmetries that do not seem to be inherent in the phenomena.*[257] He took his example of *asymmetry* from an area of study he had grown up with – electromagnetism. His father and uncle had spent their careers trying to eke a living out of the appliance of this knowledge, creating and installing dynamos and other electrical equipment. At the age of five Einstein had been fascinated by the *wonder* of a compass obeying an invisible magnetic field. In his daily work at the patent office he had to evaluate new designs of dynamos. The anomalies in the theory that explained how these technologies operated are subtle, even abstruse, yet their implications are, as Einstein alone could see, profound. They suggest a view of the universe that is strange and counter-intuitive.

Michael Faraday's discovery of electromagnetic induction in 1831 was Einstein's point of departure. Danish physicist Hans Christian Oersted (1777– 1851) had shown how an electric current flowing through a wire creates a magnetic field. Similarly, Faraday had found that moving a magnet through a loop of wire generates an electric current in the wire: 'electricity in motion produces magnetism, and magnetism in motion produces electricity.'[258] Faraday's discovery led

Michael Faraday

directly to the invention of electric generators, the core business of the Einstein family firm. But Einstein was puzzled by contradictions in the explanation of this phenomenon. Hoffmann, Einstein's former assistant, takes up the story: 'When a magnet and a loop of wire move past one another, an electric current appears in the wire. Suppose we think of the magnet as moving and the loop as at rest. Then Maxwell's theory gives an excellent explanation. Suppose we now switch and think of the coil as moving and the magnet at rest. Then Maxwell's theory again gives an excellent explanation; but it is a quite different one physically, and this even though the calculated currents are equal.'[259] The first explanation is that an electric field has been produced, whereas the second is *an electromotive force.*[260]

This is the asymmetry that Einstein found *intolerable.*[261] His paper draws our attention to the fact that our understanding of what is happening here depends on whether we view events from the perspective of the loop of wire or the magnet: *I was convinced that the difference between the two was merely a difference in the choice of the observer's position and not a real difference. Viewed from the magnet there was certainly no electric field present, but viewed from the electric circuit such a field certainly existed. Therefore the existence of the electric field was a relative one, dependent on the state of motion of the system of co-ordinates used, and only the electric and magnetic fields* together – *regardless of the state of motion of the observer or the system of co-ordinates – formed a kind of objective reality. This phenomenon of magnetoelectric induction compelled me to postulate the (special) relativity theory.*[262]

According to Newtonian mechanics an observer at rest and one in uniform motion observe the same physical laws in operation. However, as the example of electromagnetic induction shows, this did not seem to apply. Although an observer can view events from different perspectives there can be only one physical explanation of what occurred. It was now that Einstein's approach to science became crucial. He had reached a point where he was *more and more in despair about the possibility of discovering the true laws by means of constructive efforts based on known facts.*[263] An inductive method, trying to piece together facts to create a theory, was not working. So Einstein looked for a *universal formal principle,*[264] something as fundamental as thermodynamics. This principle was relativity. According to this, *the same laws of electrodynamics and optics will be valid for all co-ordinate systems in which the equations of mechanics hold.*[265] In other words, all observers moving at a constant speed will get the same results for their experiments. There could, after all, be only one physical explanation of events.

Einstein then proposed a second principle: regardless of an observer's speed, he or she will always measure the velocity of light in a vacuum to be the same – 186,000 miles per second (approximately 300,000 km/s). At first sight these two principles seem unrelated. But light, as Maxwell had shown in his brilliant theory, could be described as a wave of electricity and magnetism: 'Einstein's great insight is that electromagnetic induction is the arena in which optics, electromagnetic theory, and mechanics all overlap.'[266] Maxwell's equations in his 1864 paper 'A Dynamical Theory of the Electromagnetic Field' contain a constant (c), which stands for the speed of electromagnetic waves. It turned out that this was also the speed of light. Einstein's uniquely intuitive approach to science can

The principle of relativity began with Italian physicist and astronomer Galileo Galilei (1564–1642). In his *Dialogue on the Two Chief World Systems* (1632) Galileo used the example of an experiment conducted 'in the main cabin below decks on some large ship' moving 'with whatever velocity', provided that 'the motion be uniform and not fluctuating this way and that'. He concluded that 'not the least change in all the effects named' should occur and that 'from no one of them could you tell whether the ship is moving or not'. The experiments of the seafaring scientists would obey the same laws of physics as those conducted ashore. Although measurements of time or velocity might be relative to whether you were on ship or shore, the laws of physics were always universally true. This was an important principle in Galileo's day, at a time when scientists were struggling to grasp the implications of the idea that the ground beneath their feet was moving as the earth orbited the sun. Einstein imagined travelling at the speed of light and realised that, according to Newtonian physics, *I should observe such a beam of*

light as an electromagnetic field at rest. This meant that if you were moving at the speed of light and looked in a mirror you would see nothing, because the light from your face couldn't catch up with the mirror. But if this were so then it would violate the principle of relativity, according to which the laws of physics are the same regardless of whether an observer is at rest or moving. This was the profound paradox that led directly to the special theory of relativity.[267]

be seen in the way he selected this aspect of Maxwell's theory, raising it to the level of a fundamental principle, despite having contradicted Maxwell's notion of light as a wave in his quantum hypothesis. It required a scientific leap of faith – one that most scientists were unwilling to make. An aesthetic dimension to Einstein's theories is also apparent in his objection to *asymmetries* and his belief in the ultimate simplicity of the laws underlying nature: *A theory is the*

A LEAP OF FAITH

more impressive the greater the simplicity of its premises, the more different kinds of things it relates, and the more extended its area of applicability.[268] The mathematical expression of this sublime simplicity was for Einstein as beautiful as a Mozart sonata.

One striking result of these two principles was that the widely accepted notion of the ether became *superfluous.*[269] Maxwell's waves of electricity and magnetism rippling through space raised the question as to what medium was carrying these waves. An invisible, space-filling ether was the answer for physicists at the end of the 19th century, and it was an explanation that the young Einstein initially accepted, as shown in his first scientific essay (1895). The idea made perfect sense – a 'luminiferous' or light-bearing ether spreading through space like a sea rippling with electromagnetic waves. It also helped reconcile Maxwell's theory with Newtonian mechanics. Maxwell's theory correctly predicted the speed of light, but as speed is always relative to what it is being measured against (the reference

Maxwell explained how the ether carried his electromagnetic waves through space: 'The vast interplanetary and interstellar regions will no longer be regarded as waste places in the universe, which the Creator has not seen fit to fill with the symbols of the manifold order of His kingdom. We shall find them to be already full of this wonderful medium; so full, that no human power can remove it from the smallest portion of space, or produce the slightest flaw in its infinite continuity. It extends unbroken, from star to star; and when a molecule of hydrogen vibrates in the dog-star, the medium receives the impulses of these vibrations; and after carrying them in its immense bosom for three years, delivers them in due course, regular order, and full tale into the spectroscope of Mr Huggins, at Tulse Hill.'[270]

frame) the question had to be asked: what was Maxwell measuring the speed of light against? The speed of a tennis ball is measured relative to the racket and the player's position on the ground. The speed of water waves can be calculated with respect to the sea or (if there is an underlying current) to the shore. Similarly, scientists decided that the velocity of light waves was calculated with respect to the medium that carries them: the all-pervading ether. The ether became a universal frame of reference, *space at absolute rest*, as Einstein said.[271]

But for Einstein, *absolute rest* was untenable, an idea adopted by physicists to make Maxwell's theory conform to Newtonian physics. Faraday's example of electromagnetism offered no evidence for it. Neither did experiments to detect the motion of the earth relative to the ether, such as the Michelson-Morley experiment at the end of the 19th century, which tried unsuccessfully to find variations in the speed of light. The contrast between Faraday's experiment and the absolute value accorded to the ether in Maxwell's theory was the asymmetry that so perplexed Einstein. It offended his desire for a universal theory. To resolve this problem, he decided that the velocity of a light ray had to be the same for every observer, regardless of their speed. The ether, permeating everything and leading a *ghostly existence alongside the rest of matter*,[272] was redundant and Einstein dismissed it in a sentence. There was simply no need for it in the theory he proposed.

The notion that the velocity of light was constant contradicted the Newtonian law of the addition of velocities. If a tennis player hits a ball on board a ship we can measure its speed relative to two reference frames: the ship or the shore. The observer on the shore will measure a higher speed for a ball travelling towards the front of the ship. The difference will be exactly the speed of the ship. But if we do the same experiment with a light ray then, according to Einstein, the speed of the ship will have no effect. The speed of light is constant: Einstein had discovered a new fundamental principle in the universe.

By so doing Einstein toppled the twin pillars of Newtonian

mechanics: the absolutes of space and time. In the *Principia* (1687) Newton states: 'Absolute, true, and mathematical time, of itself and from its own nature, flows equably [equally] without relation to anything external. [. . .] Absolute space, in its own nature, without relation to anything external, remains always similar and immovable.'[273] In Einstein's theory there was no ether-filled 'absolute space'; all motion was relative to an individual's frame of reference. Many years after the special theory of relativity appeared, Einstein felt the need to apologise for challenging the father of physics: *Newton, forgive me; you found just about the only way possible in your age for a man of highest reasoning and creative power.*[274] Of course, in the everyday world Newton's laws remain valid. It is only at extremely high velocities approaching the speed of light that his laws are observed to break down, in particle physics for example. It was clear, however, that a new age had dawned, heralded by an unknown clerk in the Bern patent office.

One implication of Einstein's second principle is that our idea of simultaneous events is an illusion. There is no such thing as a universal 'now'. Light takes time to travel, so that a star we see tonight in the night sky may no longer exist by the time its light reaches our planet. It is not possible to say that events occurring in one reference frame (for example on earth) happen at the same time as they do on another (the star). The universe is in a real sense no longer a whole, but must be viewed as a multitude of fragments, each one locked into its own space-time.

There are other, stranger implications of making the speed of light a universal constant. If a spaceship were chasing a ray of light, as in Einstein's original thought experiment in Aarau, we would still measure the speed of light relative to the spaceship's frame of reference at 300,000 km/s, even if the spaceship were moving at 299,000 km/s. According to Newton it should be a mere 1,000 km/s. Einstein's theory predicts other bizarre effects at speeds approaching the velocity of light. For instance, an observer will see objects moving at such speeds contracted in the direction of the motion: a ruler would shrink and the round face of a watch would become oval shaped, but still keep ticking regularly. This is no mere optical illusion, but it would not damage the instruments. At such extreme speeds space itself contracts. Two spaceships passing each other at a speed approaching that of a ray of light would see each other's ship contracted and yet would see nothing changed within their own ship. Which ship really did shrink then? The answer is perplexing but provides a clue to the purpose of Einstein's principle: both ships can be said to have shrunk in relation to the other ship's frame of reference. But in their own frames of reference they remain unchanged. There is no absolute point from which measurements are taken – all motion is relative. In his principle of relativity, Einstein was concerned with laying down rules about how we know the universe around us. A vital part of this is the inclusion of time as well as space in our measurements.

'Suppose this tram were moving away from that clock on the very beam with which we see what the clock says. [. . .] Suppose the clock behind me says "noon" when I leave. I now travel 186,000 miles away from it at the speed of light; that ought to take me one second. But the time on the clock, as I see it, still says "noon", because it takes the beam of light from the clock exactly as long as it has taken me. So far as the clock as I see it, so far as the universe inside the tram is concerned, in keeping up with the speed of light I have cut myself off from the passage of time. [. . .] Einstein's is a man's eye view, in which what you see and what I see is relative to each of us, that is, to our place and speed. And this relativity cannot be removed. We cannot know what the world is like in itself, we can only compare what it looks like to each of us, by the practical procedure of exchanging messages. I in my tram and you in your chair can share no divine and instant view of events – we can only communicate our own views to one another. And communication is not instant; we cannot remove from it the basic time-lag of all signals, which is set by the speed of light.'

JACOB BRONOWSKI,
The Ascent of Man[275]

Just as space contracts at high velocities, so time slows. Clocks as well as the beating of our hearts all slow down. For the traveller, time seems to be passing normally. But for the observer back on earth,

ALL MOTION IS RELATIVE

time for an astronaut moving at speeds approaching that of light will slow and the traveller will age more slowly. As in the example of the two spaceships observing each other, the astronaut will see the clocks on earth slowing down.

An apparent paradox regarding this was once put to Einstein. If a twin remains on earth while the other twin travels through space, both perceive the other's time frame to have slowed but their own to remain unchanged. But when the travelling twin returns to earth who will have aged slower? The answer is that the travelling twin has in fact aged less than the twin on earth. Indeed, this is an experiment that has been confirmed with clocks placed on satellites.

As well as space and time, mass is also a relative property: an object will gain in mass as it approaches the speed of light. Reaching the speed of light is impossible, for then an object's mass would be infinite, its space would contract to virtually nothing and time would stop. Scientists using particle accelerators, such as CERN (the Organization for Nuclear Research) in Geneva, have experienced the practical implications of this. As they pump more energy into particles to make them go faster, the increase in speed declines. It's a law of diminishing returns. The extra energy increases the particle's mass, making it more difficult for it to accelerate. This link between energy and mass was another striking result of Einstein's relativity paper, one which he formulated some months later at the end of September. Published in the *Annalen* on 21 November, this short paper was Einstein's fifth in 1905 and formed the basis for the most famous scientific equation ever written: $E=mc^2$.

In late summer 1905, Einstein wrote to his friend Habicht com-plaining that *the value of my time does not weigh heavily these days; there aren't always subjects that are ripe for rumination. At least none that are really exciting.*[277] It is an extraordinary comment, given the originality of the papers he had written just a few weeks before. But one matter *did cross my mind*, he adds with remarkable understatement: *Namely, the relativity principle, in association with Maxwell's fundamental equations, requires that the mass be a direct measure of the energy contained in a body; light carries mass with it. A noticeable reduction of mass would have to take place in the case of radium. The consideration is amusing and seductive; but for all I know, God Almighty might be laughing at the whole matter and might have been leading me around by the nose.*[278] This was the germ of an idea that eventually became a three-page paper called 'Does the Inertia of a Body Depend on its Energy Content?' The title in the form of a question indicates the tentative nature of Einstein's ideas at this stage. In it he suggested that *if a body emits the energy L in the form of radiation, its mass decreases by L/V^2.*[279] As in his paper on relativity, he used L to denote energy (*lebendige Kraft* or 'vital energy') and V (velocity) the speed of light. Expressed in terms now familiar throughout the world, energy (E) released in the form of light (c) results in a reduction in mass (m) by an amount E/c^2. His far-reaching conclusion was that *the mass of a body is a measure of its energy content.*[280]

The implications of this occupied Einstein for the next two years and in May 1907 he published a paper in which he used the now-famous equation $E=mc^2$ expressing the equivalence of mass and energy. It took 25 years before his theory was demonstrated in the laboratory. But it was the discovery of nuclear fission in 1938 that showed the world how to release the enormous reservoir of energy locked up inside matter. When the atomic bomb was dropped on Hiroshima on 6 August 1945, about one gram of the mass of the bomb produced energy equivalent to more than 12,000 tons of explosive. As Einstein realised, such knowledge brought with it a *great threat of evil* and by 1946 averting that threat had become *the most urgent problem of our time.*[281]

When he finished writing his first paper on relativity, Einstein was so mentally exhausted that he went to bed for two weeks. Mileva had 'helped him solve certain mathematical problems' and had 'checked

$E = M C^2$

Einstein at his desk in the Swiss Patent Office, Bern, 1905

the article again and again' before mailing it.[282] It was, she said, 'a very beautiful piece of work'.[283] Some have claimed that what Einstein referred to in 1901 as *our work on relative motion* was a joint effort with his wife,[284] but although Mileva probably helped with the calculations as well as finding data and writing up his notes, the main creative inspiration was Einstein's. However, he did credit one person with helping him: Michele Besso. In the paper he said Besso *steadfastly stood by me in my work on the problem discussed here, and [. . .] I am indebted to him for several valuable suggestions.*[285]

In late summer 1905, Mileva finally convinced her husband to make the long train journey to meet her parents. They went first to Belgrade where they stayed with Mileva's best friend, Helene Savić. After a week Einstein, Mileva, and little Hans Albert travelled to her parents' home on Kisaćka Street in Novi Sad. It is not known if Einstein finally met Lieserl, who would have been three and a half years old, or even if she was still alive. Mileva proudly informed her parents that Einstein's work that summer would make him world famous, and it is unlikely Mrs Marić gave her son-in-law the thrashing she had once promised him.

The Happiest Thought of My Life
1906 – 1915

On his 27th birthday in 1906, Einstein learned that he was to be promoted to the position of Technical Expert Second Class and his salary raised by 600 francs to 4,500 francs. According to his boss, he was one of 'the most prized experts in the agency'.[286] Writing to his friend Solovine, Einstein reported: *The three of us are fine, as always. The little sprout has grown into quite an imposing, impertinent fellow. As for my science, I am not all that successful at present. Soon I will reach the age of stagnation and sterility when one laments the revolutionary spirit of the young.*[287] According to the biographer and physicist Abraham Pais 'no one before or since has widened the horizons of physics in so short a time as Einstein did in 1905,' and yet, barely a year later, Einstein was complaining about his lack of success.[288] However, other physicists were beginning to take notice, in particular Max Planck, who was to win the Nobel Prize for physics in 1918. Planck played a key role in promoting the theories of this unknown patent office clerk, encouraging his assistant Max von Laue (1879–1960) to work on relativity. In 1911 Laue published the first book on the subject.

When Laue visited Einstein in August 1907, he naturally assumed that he taught at Bern University. When he eventually found his way to the patent office, he reports that 'the young man who came to meet me made so unexpected an impression on me that I did not believe he could possibly be the father of the relativity theory.'[289] Laue recalled how he stood with Einstein on the bridge over the River Aare discussing relativity and looking at the magnificent view of the Bernese Oberland. Einstein offered him one of his cheap cigars but Laue found it so unpleasant that he 'accidentally' dropped it into the river.[290] Although unimpressed by Einstein's choice of cigar, Laue had no doubts about the quality of his mind. 'He is a revolutionary,' he wrote to fellow physicist Jakob Laub (1882–1962). 'In the first two hours of the conversation he overturned all of mechanics and electrodynamics, and this on the basis of statistics.'[291]

Despite his promotion, Einstein was no longer satisfied with his work as a *respectable Federal ink pisser*.[292] Jakob Laub, who visited Einstein in 1908, said tactlessly that he was 'surprised to read that you must sit in an office for eight hours a day. History is full of bad jokes.'[293] Einstein had in fact tried to find an academic position in June 1907, but his application to lecture at Bern University was turned down. To add insult to injury, the Professor of Physics, Aimé Forster (1843–1926), returned Einstein's relativity paper with the comment 'I can't understand a word of what you've written here.'[294] A subsequent application, which Einstein supported with a paper on his current work into radiation, was more successful and in 1908 he became a *Privatdozent* at the University of Bern, an unsalaried position that entitled a researcher to offer courses. He gave his inaugural lecture, 'On the Limit of the Validity of Classical Thermodynamics', in February. Unfortunately his physics course did not prove popular. In fact, only three people enrolled and they were Einstein's friends. The following semester only one student turned up and Einstein cancelled his course.

It was not until May 1909 that he finally found a full-time academic post. Alfred Kleiner (1849–1916), Professor of Experimental Physics at Zurich University, wanted to appoint a theoretical physicist, but Einstein was not his first choice and Kleiner was distinctly unimpressed by one of his Bern lectures. Einstein 'holds monologues', he said, and was 'a long way from being a teacher'.[295] But Einstein convinced him to attend another lecture, this time in Zurich. *I was lucky*, wrote Einstein to Laub. *Contrary to my habit, I lectured well on that occasion*.[296] In 1908 his old mathematics professor, Hermann

Minkowski, had painted a vivid picture of the new relativistic universe implied by his former student's theory: 'From now on space by itself, and time by itself, are destined to fade into mere shadows, and only a kind of union of the two will preserve an independent reality.'[297] Einstein's ideas were beginning to make waves in physics and this rather than his lecturing abilities is what finally persuaded Kleiner. On 7 May 1909 the 30-year-old Einstein was appointed Extraordinary Professor of Theoretical Physics at the University of Zurich. He was, as he told Laub with characteristic wit, finally *an official member of the guild of whores.*[298]

In September 1909 Einstein attended the annual Congress of German Natural Scientists and Physicians, his first international science conference. He told his audience, including Planck, that the ether was *obsolete* and that *a profound change in our views on the nature and constitution of light is imperative.*[299] In his lecture, Einstein anticipated the work of quantum theorists like Danish nuclear physicist Niels Bohr (1885–1962) in the 1920s, who would seek to explain how light can

Einstein attends a meeting of the German Physical Society, 1909

MAKING WAVES

behave as both a wave and a particle: *It is [. . .] my opinion that the next stage in the development of theoretical physics will bring us a theory of light that can be understood as a kind of fusion of the wave and emission* [i.e. quantum] *theories of light*.[300] According to the Austrian-born physicist Wolfgang Pauli (1900–58), this lecture was 'one of the turning points in the evolution of theoretical physics',[301] and represented Einstein's acceptance into the ranks of elite physicists.

In October the Einsteins moved out of their Bern apartment at 53 Aergertenstrasse, where they had lived since spring 1906. In Zurich they lived at 12 Moussonstrasse, overlooking the city and a few minutes walk from the Institute of Physics in Rämistrasse. Once again, they were back in the *beautiful surroundings of Zurich,*[302] only now Einstein was no longer a student, but a professor. In the month that Einstein began teaching at Zurich University, Wilhelm Ostwald nominated him for a Nobel Prize. It would be more than a decade, however, before the committee felt able to bestow this honour on Einstein.

Einstein's position within the scientific community was now assured. The insecurity of earlier years was forgotten and colleagues noticed a new confidence in him. Physicist and pacifist Friedrich Adler (1879–1960), who lived in the apartment below them, wrote that Einstein had the most independent mind in physics: 'The majority of scientists don't even understand his approach.'[303] Mileva told Helene proudly: 'He is now counted among the leading German-speaking physicists and is being frightfully courted. I am very happy about his success, which he has really earned; I only hope and wish that fame does not exert a detrimental influence on his human side.'[304]

As this letter suggests, once again Einstein and Mileva's relationship had entered stormy waters. In 1899 he had a brief holiday romance with a woman called Anna Schmid. He wrote her a flirtatious poem in which he kissed her *on the tiny little mouth*.[305] When Anna read of his appointment at Zurich she wrote to him and replying in May 1909 Einstein recalled the *lovely weeks* they spent together.

He felt certain that she had *become as exquisite and cheerful a woman today as you were a lovely and joyful young girl in those days.* He concluded tersely *Miss Marić has indeed become my wife.*[306] In a postscript he gave the now married Anna the address of the Institute for Physics in Zurich and suggested she contact him there.

Anna's reply was found by Mileva who immediately suspected the two were having an affair and wrote to Anna's husband, complaining about her 'inappropriate letter'.[307] Forced to explain things to her husband, Einstein exonerated Anna and blamed his own *careless behaviour* and Mileva's *extreme jealousy*.[308] The incident cast a shadow over their already troubled marriage. In November, Einstein complained to his friend Besso about the lack of time for research, adding darkly: *mental balance lost because of M[ileva] not regained.*[309] Even in 1951, the scars from this incident had still not healed. In a letter to Anna's daughter, Einstein wrote bitterly that Mileva's jealousy was to be expected from a woman of such *uncommon ugliness.*[310]

Mileva's letters to Helene reveal that she was feeling 'very starved for love' and blaming 'wicked science': 'You see, with such fame, not much time remains for his wife.' She ends poignantly: 'the pearls are given to one, to the other the case.'[311] Einstein did not bring very high expectations to his relationships, and once told a woman friend: *What a strange thing must be a girl's soul! Do you really believe that you could find permanent happiness through others, even if this be the one and only beloved man?*[312] Instead, he longed to escape from the realm of *personal hopes, wishes and desires* into the objectivity of science.[313] He agreed with Schopenhauer's view that great scientists and artists were united in their *flight from daily life* and their need to free themselves from *the shackles of one's ever-changing desires.*[314] The *escape from personal existence into the world of objective perception and understanding* was a defining motive for Einstein, and one that had a profound effect on his relationships with women.[315]

On 28 July 1910 Mileva gave birth to their second son, Eduard, known in the family as Tete. A friend at Zurich describes Einstein's

THE FLIGHT FROM DAILY LIFE

unusual approach to childcare: 'The door of the flat was open to allow the floor which had just been scrubbed, as well as the washing hung up in the hall, to dry. I entered Einstein's room. He was calmly philosophic, with one hand rocking the bassinet in which there was a child. In his mouth Einstein had a bad, a very bad cigar, and in the other hand an open book. The stove was smoking horribly. How in the world could he bear it?'[316]

At the university Einstein earned the same modest salary as at the patent office. But he knew it to be a stepping-stone to greater things and within months of starting he was approached by the German University in Prague about a professorship. Planck had been consulted by the chairman of the appointment committee, Anton Lampa, and had praised Einstein as a new Copernicus. In order to qualify for the appointment, Einstein had to state for the first time that he was a Jew. He had always described himself officially as 'without religious denomination'; but he did not regard it as a significant step. *Returning to the bosom of Abraham meant nothing to me*, he wrote later. *A piece of paper that had to be signed.*[317]

The final offer from Prague was 8,672 Austrian crowns, double his salary at Zurich. Once news leaked out that he might leave Zurich, his students petitioned the Department of Education, praising Einstein's 'amazing talent for presenting the most difficult problems of theoretical physics so clearly'.[318] As one of the signatories of the petition said, this unconventional professor 'in his rather shabby attire with trousers too short for him' had 'captured our hearts'.[319] Students liked the relaxed atmosphere in Einstein's lectures, which usually ended with the question: *Who's coming along to the Café Terrasse?*[320] His popularity earned him a salary increase of 1,000 francs effective

Polish astronomer Nicolaus Copernicus (1473–1543) developed the modern theory of the solar system. He noticed that it was easier to calculate planetary positions by adopting a system in which the earth revolved around the sun (instead of Ptolemy's system in which the earth was at the centre of the universe). This novel theory upset many long-cherished beliefs about man's privileged place in the cosmos.

from October 1910, but by September it was certain he would go to Prague.

Einstein spent his last few months in Zurich working on a theory of opalescence – an explanation of why the sky appears blue during the day and red in early morning and evening. He showed that the colour of the sky was caused by gas molecules in the air scattering the sun's light. It was a further attempt to convince doubters such as Mach of the reality of atoms. He was satisfied with the resulting article: *I take great pleasure in it*, he told Laub.[321] In January 1911, just before going to Prague, Einstein received an invitation from one of his scientific heroes, Hendrik Antoon Lorentz, to lecture at Leiden in the Netherlands. Even at this early stage in his career Einstein confessed *I don't like this public lecturing*.[322] But the possibility of meeting Lorentz and discussing the *radiation problem* made him accept the offer to *appear on stage*.[323] Einstein regarded Lorentz as an intellectual father figure, commenting: *For me personally, he meant more than all the others I have met on my life's journey*.[324] For once, Mileva was able to travel with him on 8 February, as her mother was staying in

Once when closing time at the Café Terrasse threatened to interrupt their discussions, he invited the students back to his apartment, telling them: *This morning I received some work from Planck in which there must be a mistake. We could read it together.* As he made them coffee, they tried to spot the error. Hans Tanner, Einstein's doctoral student, takes up the story: 'After a quarter of an hour our host returned with some steaming coffee and asked: *Well, have you found the mistake?* "You must be mistaken, Herr Professor," I replied, "there is no mistake in it." *Yes, there is, for otherwise that and that would become that and that.* It was a simple dimensional datum that he pointed out to us. This was his strong point. Behind a formula he immediately saw the physical content, while for us it remained only an abstract formula. After five minutes we scratched our heads. How could we have been so foolish not to have sensed the source of the mistake? "Now let's write to Professor Planck in Berlin," I suggested, "and tell him of the mistake he made." *A good idea. But we won't write and tell him that he's made a mistake. The result is correct, but the proof is faulty. We'll simply write and tell him how the real proof should run. The main thing is the content, not the mathematics. With mathematics one can prove anything.*'[325]

AN INTELLECTUAL FATHER FIGURE

Zurich and so could look after the children. Einstein sent a postcard to Adler: *If the house burns down, or some other nice thing like that happens, please send us a wire to the address of Prof H A Lorentz, Leiden.*[326]

Einstein and his family arrived in Prague in March 1911 and by April they had moved into an apartment at what is now Lesnická 7 in the Smichov district. Mileva did not want to leave Zurich. In fact their stay in the historic city was shorter than either of them imagined and before the year was over a new offer of an academic position was on the table. Life in Prague became something of an ordeal for Einstein. He complained constantly about the *never-ending paperwork*, the *Czech language, bedbugs* and the *awful water* – the tap-water was brown and undrinkable.[327] Fleas were another domestic hazard: 'A fire broke out in the maid's room one night. Einstein rushed in with a bucket of water. He was there for only a few minutes but when he came out he was crawling with fleas and had to take a bath.'[328] Mileva was worried about the children catching diseases; bubonic plague and typhoid were not unheard of in Prague at this time. *The air is full of soot, the water life-threatening, the people superficial, shallow, and rough,* kvetched Einstein,[329] although he did concede that Prague was full of *architectural beauties.*[330] There were some advantages: they had a live-in maid and for the first time a flat with electricity.

One of the first women in Prague to go to university, Berta Fanta's famous Tuesday evening at-homes were the place to be. A cosmopolitan elite flocked to her house in the Old Town Square, including the mathematician Gerhard Kowalewski and the physicist Philipp Frank.

Although he attended Bertha Fanta's famed soirées, where he met Prague's Jewish intellectuals such as the writers Franz Kafka (1883–1924) and Max Brod (1884–1968) – who later used Einstein as the model for Kepler in his novel *The Redemption of Tycho Brahe* (1916) – Einstein felt intellectually isolated in Prague. In 1911 Einstein was still working on his *quantum hypothesis* and he told Besso: *I no longer ask whether these quanta really exist.*[331] Einstein enjoyed drawing visitors' attention to the view from his office window which overlooked the garden of an insane asylum: *Those are the madmen who do not occupy themselves with quantum theory,* he would say with a droll expression.[332] In June he received an invitation to speak at an international conference sponsored by the wealthy Belgian industrial chemist Ernest Solvay (1838–1922). Participants included Walther Nernst, Henri Poincaré, Planck, and Lorentz, as well as the renowned chemist Marie Curie (1867–1934), who discovered radium, and the physicist Ernest Rutherford (1871–1937), who would succeed in splitting the atom in 1918. It was to be the first of many influential Solvay Congresses on the state of physics.

By the end of 1911 Einstein had two offers of chairs in physics, one from the University of Utrecht, the other from his alma mater in Zurich. Poincaré gave Einstein a glowing recommendation: 'The future will show, more and more, the value of Einstein, and the university which is intelligent enough to capture this young scholar is certain to reap great honour.'[333] Einstein was not so preoccupied by physics that he was unaware that he had become a valuable academic commodity. He ruthlessly played one university off against the other, in order to negotiate a higher salary from Zurich. The deal was wrapped up by February 1912, with the Swiss government agreeing

The Solvay Congress, 1911. Einstein (second from right) stands next to Paul Langevin. Ernest Rutherford stands behind Marie Curie

A VALUABLE COMMODITY

to pay him 1,000 francs a year more than Prague, an exceptional amount. Einstein could not conceal his excitement about returning to Zurich, telling his Swiss friends Alfred and Clara Stern: *Two days ago I was appointed to the Polytechnic in Zurich (hallelujah!) and I have already submitted my imperial royal resignation here. We old folks and the two baby bears are immensely happy about it, so that I simply had to send you the news. We will pull out of here this summer already.*[334]

The *baby bears* were their sons Hans Albert and Eduard. In March 1912 Einstein reported on their progress: *Our bear cubs are a great joy to us, and the older one is already trying, with some measure of success, to become a proper bear. For example, he has already started to learn to play the piano, and he does it with great zeal. I'm working at full speed on a problem (gravitation).*[335] As usual in Einstein's correspondence, his scientific research is mentioned in the same breath as personal matters, in this case a tantalising reference to his work on gravity, a problem that had occupied him since 1907. Also in March he wrote to Besso: *I have been working like mad on the gravitation problem.*[336] But Einstein had run into difficulties. As Professor Minkowski (who died in 1909) had often complained, Einstein was never strong on maths. Once back in Zurich, his friend Marcel Grossmann, now professor of mathematics at the Poly, would give him the mathematical help he needed to develop his revolutionary new theory.

His return to Zurich was fixed for the late summer of 1912 and he couldn't wait to leave. In Easter Einstein visited Berlin *to talk shop with various people* including Nernst, Planck, and the chemist Fritz Haber (1868–1934).[337] While there he also met his cousin Elsa Löwenthal (née Einstein), whom he had not seen since they were children. Elsa, now divorced, lived with her two daughters Ilse and Margot in an apartment above her parents, Rudolf and Fanny Einstein, at 5 Haberlandstrasse, Berlin. Blonde, blue-eyed Elsa was very different from Mileva. She was lively, keen on socialising and gave poetry readings in the theatre. At home Mileva would often sink into long periods of silence that irritated her husband. Later Einstein said that she was *distrustful, short on words and depressive, that is, gloomy*. He put it down to a *schizophrenic genetic disposition coming from her mother's family*.[338] There can be little doubt that Einstein's mother had told Elsa all about his troubled marriage. After a trip to the Wannsee, a Berlin lake, the two fell in love. *I suffer very much because I'm not allowed to love truly*, Einstein told her.[339]

At the end of his life Einstein admitted that *the marriage, entered by me from a sense of duty and against the passionate opposition of my parents, was unhappy – for which Mileva by no means bore the main responsibility. With an inner resistance I had undertaken something that simply exceeded my strength*.[340] Meeting Elsa convinced him that something had to change. Einstein was characteristically frank in his letters to Elsa when he returned to Prague at the end of April 1912, confessing that he found Mileva, his mother and sister *quite unlikable*.[341] *I have to have someone to love*, he told her, *otherwise life is miserable. And this someone is you.* However, he hotly denied Elsa's assertion that he was henpecked.[342] To avoid repeating the Anna Schmid episode, Elsa insisted he destroy her letters as soon as he had read them. He wished they lived nearer, but thought *the chances of my getting a call to Berlin are, unfortunately, rather slight*.[343] For once Einstein was wrong.

The Einsteins left Prague on 25 July 1912. On his return to Zurich, Einstein visited Grossmann for a maths lesson, as he told physicist Arnold Sommerfeld in October: *I am now working exclusively on the gravitation problem and believe that I can overcome all difficulties with the help of a mathematician friend of mine here. But one thing is certain: never before in my life have I troubled myself over anything so much, and I have gained enormous respect for mathematics, whose more subtle parts I considered until now, in my ignorance, as pure luxury! Compared with this problem, the original theory of relativity is child's play*.[344] As Einstein and Grossmann struggled to devise the complex field equations to explain gravity, Mileva complained to Helene that he now had little time for her or the children. The resulting paper was finished in May 1913, although Einstein was convinced that his *superhuman effort* had solved the *gravitation problem*,[345] it turned out to be only a partial solution. It was not until 1915 that he would have the final theory.

On 14 July 1913 Einstein wrote a postcard to Elsa with *some really good news*:[346] Planck and Nernst had offered him membership of the prestigious Prussian Academy of Sciences and a research professorship at the University of Berlin. The salary was generous – 12,000 marks a year. For that he would not even be expected to teach – he would be *totally free*.[347] To a friend he admitted his doubts: *These Berlin people are speculating with me as if I were a prize hen. But I don't know whether I can still lay eggs.*[348] Nevertheless it was, as he admitted to Elsa, a *colossal honour*.[349]

Later Einstein claimed it was Elsa who *drew me to Berlin in the first place*.[350] His relationship with Mileva had deteriorated badly and she was reluctant to go to Berlin where she would be closer to Einstein's relatives, especially his mother. Einstein discussed the possibility of a divorce with Elsa: *I treat my wife as an employee whom I cannot fire. I have my own bedroom and avoid being alone with her. In this form I can endure the 'living together' quite well.*[351] Despite Mileva's misgivings they left Zurich in March 1914. Einstein went first to Leiden to lecture on his theories of gravity while Mileva stayed in Locarno for three weeks with the boys. Three-year-old Eduard had been ill throughout the winter with *whooping cough, a middle-ear infection, and the flu,* and was *very run down*.[352] The doctor prescribed a dose of warm spring weather in the canton of Ticino near the Alps to help him recover. Cynically, Einstein commented: *This has its good side. For Miza must go with him, and I will be alone in Berlin for some time.*[353]

Einstein's move to Berlin represents a watershed in his life. He was to remain there for almost 20 years, during which time he would become world famous, a celebrity whose every word was reported to an eager public. Soon he would look back nostalgically on his life in Switzerland as a time of innocent freedom. In his personal life, too, Berlin brought big changes. Within months of arriving, Einstein's marriage was effectively over.

The separation was acrimonious and painful. For the few months he and Mileva were together in Berlin, Einstein spent most of his time working at the Academy or with his relatives. Weeks went by without Mileva knowing where he was, although she suspected he was with Elsa. In July they argued and Einstein moved out of their apartment. His friend, Fritz Haber, acted as go-between and Einstein drew up an extraordinary list of conditions that Mileva had to agree to if they were to continue living together:

Conditions.

A. *You make sure*

  1) that my clothes and laundry are kept in good order and repair

  2) that I receive my three meals regularly in my room.

  3) That my bedroom and office are always kept neat, in particular, that the desk is available to me alone.

B. *You renounce all personal relations with me as far as maintaining them is not absolutely required for social reasons. Specifically, you do without*

  1) my sitting at home with you

  2) my going out or travelling together with you.

C. *In your relations with me you commit yourself explicitly to adhering to the following points:*

  1) You are neither to expect intimacy from me nor to reproach me in any way.

  2) You must desist immediately from addressing me if I request it.

  3) You must leave my bedroom or office immediately without protest if I so request.

D. *You commit yourself not to disparage me either in word or deed in front of my children.*[354]

Surprisingly, Mileva agreed, but their relationship could not last under such conditions. On 24 July the couple drew up terms of separation. Einstein would give Mileva 5,600 marks a year (7,000 Swiss francs) and she would look after the boys in Zurich (Mileva refused to allow them to be brought up by Einstein's relatives who had been so hostile towards her). Five days later Einstein said farewell to his family at the train station. He cried so violently that Haber had to help him home. He complained to Elsa that Mileva would turn his sons against him and he wrote long letters to his children, encouraging them in their studies. For her part, Elsa pressed him to finalise the divorce so they could be married, but Einstein was reluctant to take the final step. The following year he wrote to a friend: *Life without my wife is a veritable rebirth for me personally. It feels as if I had ten years of prison behind me.*[355] Indeed, he was in no hurry to marry again, as he told Elsa: *Is it a fear of the comfortable life, of nice furniture, or [. . .] even of becoming some sort of contented bourgeois? I myself don't know.*[356] Einstein packed up the contents of their Dahlem apartment, sent them to Mileva and rented a small bachelor pad: *I have kept only very little for myself, namely the blue sofa, the rustic table, two beds (originating from my mother's household), the desk, the small chest of drawers from my grandparents' household, unfortunately also the electrical lamp you want, not knowing that you are attached to it.*[357]

Einstein was appalled when war broke out in autumn 1914. Without hesitation he signed an anti-war petition drawn up by a colleague – in the prevailing jingoistic atmosphere only three other academics dared to sign it. In a short article, 'My Opinion of the War', Einstein argued that *the psychological roots of war are [. . .] biologically founded in the aggressive characteristics of the male creature.*[358] He also voiced his belief in international co-operation as the way forward, calling for a European government. From now on Einstein would remain firmly internationalist in his politics, a view only confirmed by the devastation wrought by two world wars. He was disgusted by the patriotic sentiments of his German colleagues, many of whom, like Haber, were working on terrible new weapons such as poison gas. It was like living in a *madhouse*, he said bluntly.[359]

One immediate effect of the war was that a German expedition to Russia to observe the solar eclipse was arrested and imprisoned. The expedition had set out to test Einstein's hypothesis that gravity was not a force, as Newton thought, but a field. In his 1911 paper 'On the Influence of Gravitation on the Propagation of Light', Einstein outlined a test for this: *according to the theory I am going to set forth, rays of light passing near the sun experience a deflection by its gravitational field, so that a fixed star appearing near the sun displays an apparent increase of its angular distance from the latter, which amounts to almost one second of arc.*[360] At the end of his paper he challenged astronomers to test his *adventurous* theory during an eclipse, when stars near the sun were visible. It was lucky for Einstein that the Russian expedition failed; his theory was still in its early stages and in fact his calculations were wrong.

The application of relativity to gravity was Einstein's most daunting problem to date. *The work on gravitation progresses, but at the cost of extraordinary efforts; gravitation is coy and unyielding!* To this he added that *the search is hell!*[361] Throughout the autumn and winter of 1915, he worked tirelessly on his theory. Almost the only people he wrote to were his family in Switzerland and the mathematician David Hilbert (1862–1943), who was also working on gravity. One of the riddles Einstein hoped to solve was an anomaly in the orbit of Mercury first noticed in 1859, which seemed to defy Newtonian mechanics. Banesh Hoffmann explains that Mercury's 'perihelion, the point of its orbit nearest the sun, was observed to advance by just under 5,600 seconds of arc per century, and, although most of this could be accounted for, one way or another, on Newtonian grounds, a residual increase of somewhere between 40 and 50 seconds of arc per century remained unexplained.'[362]

After many a false dawn when he thought he had solved the problem, Einstein finally had the answer in November 1915. His general theory of relativity, which he announced to the Prussian Academy of Sciences, successfully explained the perihelion advance of 43 seconds of arc per century. The years of patient and meticulous science had paid off. *I was beside myself with joy and excitement for days*, Einstein wrote to Ehrenfest in January 1916.[363] It was a 'great work of art', according to German physicist Max Born (1882–1970), 'the greatest feat of human thinking about nature, the most amazing combination of philosophical penetration, physical intuition, and mathematic skill.'[364]

The original inspiration for the general theory of relativity came in 1907, as Einstein recalled later: *I was sitting in the patent office in Bern when all of a sudden a thought occurred to me: if a person falls freely, he won't feel his own weight. I was startled. This simple thought made a deep impression on me. It impelled me toward a theory of gravitation.*[365] It was, he said, *the happiest thought of my life*, revealing the true nature of gravity: *For an observer falling freely from the roof of a house there exists [. . .] no gravitational field.*[366] This insight led Einstein in 1912 to the equivalence principle, which derives from the moment when acceleration and gravity are equal. At this point acceleration cancels out gravity and the falling person is weightless, in free fall. In another graphic illustration of physical principles, Einstein imagined a person in a lift whose cable had been severed. The person falling in the lift would be weightless. A beam of light passing from one side of the lift to the other would appear to be bent, because in the time it takes to travel through the lift, the other wall will have accelerated. True to Einstein's belief in unifying principles, the equivalence principle says that if light is bent by acceleration, then it is also bent by gravity. Hence the prediction that starlight would be bent close to the sun.

In 1907 Einstein had lacked the mathematical framework needed to develop his theory. Minkowski's four-dimensional space-time continuum, which he described a year later, was part of the answer, as was mathematician Bernhard Riemann's work on curved surfaces, which Grossmann explained to Einstein. Thanks to Grossmann, Einstein realised he needed to use a form of calculus known as tensor theory to complete his theory of gravity. To do this he drew on the work of mathematicians such as Riemann (1826–66), Bruno Christoffel (1829–1900), Gregorio Ricci (1853–1925), and Tullio Levi-Cività (1873–1941).

In Einstein's final theory, 'gravitation was not treated as a force but as an intrinsic curvature of space-time. Small bodies such as the planets moved in orbits around the sun not because the sun attracted them but because in the curved space-time around the sun there simply were no straight world lines.'[367] Newton's idea of gravity as an instantaneous force of attraction between bodies was untenable in Einstein's relativistic universe, expressed in terms of field theory. Large objects, such as planets, warp the geometry of space, as physicist John Wheeler describes: 'Space tells matter how to move and matter tells space how to curve. Gravity is not a foreign and physical force acting through space – it's a manifestation of the geometry of space right where the mass is.'[368]

Einstein's gravitational field equations governing space-time curvature are very complex: there are ten of them and 'if written out in full instead of in the compact tensor notation, they would fill a huge book with intricate symbols. And there is something about them that is intensely beautiful and almost miraculous.'[369] They did not just explain the anomalous orbit of Mercury, but also made predictions: gravitational red shift was one, whereby light passing a substantial object such as a planet will redden. Similarly, a clock near such an object will run slower than one far away from it. Einstein's idea of curved space near massive planetary bodies, such as the sun, also predicted the deflection of light. But in comparison to his earlier faulty calculations, Einstein's theory now predicted that rays of starlight passing near the sun would be deflected by 1.7 seconds of arc, double his 1911 estimate.

Einstein's equations also suggested that the universe was expanding, an idea that contradicted conventional ideas of a static universe. This was too revolutionary even for Einstein and to correct it he added what became known as a *cosmological constant* into his equations in 1917.[370] Einstein remarked later that it was 'the biggest blunder he ever made in his life'.[371] At the end of the 1920s, American astronomer Edwin Hubble (1889–1953) demonstrated that the universe was indeed expanding and, stripped of their cosmological constant, Einstein's equations later provided mathematical foundations for the Big Bang theory of the origin of the universe. Within the last few years, however, Einstein's cosmological constant has made something of a come-back, as scientists have tried to explain the presence of an anti-gravity force controlling the expansion of the universe.

According to physicist Jocelyn Bell Burnell (b.1943), 'Einstein set up quite a lot of theory [. . .] and then basically scarpered off and left other people to prove it. Since then physicists have been pretty busy gradually ticking off one by one the various bits of Einstein's theory. It is standing up very well.'[372] In the 1960s she was part of the Cambridge team that discovered pulsars, neutron stars that emit radio waves. Using a system of two neutron stars orbiting one another (a binary pulsar) it has been possible to test the accuracy of Einstein's general theory of relativity, which predicts that the stars will move closer to each other as the system loses energy in the form of gravitational radiation. The observations of this system represent a 'glorious confirmation' of general relativity, according to Bell Burnell.

The year 1915 witnessed both terrible and beautiful uses of science – Fritz Haber's poison gas was first deployed as a weapon and Einstein's general theory of relativity revolutionised our concept of gravity. From the end of 1915 to spring 1917 Einstein entered an extraordinarily productive period in his scientific career, during which he wrote a scientific paper every month. He later described the evolution of his scientific theories to Carl Seelig, using the analogy of a building. The first storey was special relativity, the second general relativity, which extended the theory to include gravity. The third storey was the one which Einstein devoted the rest of his life to constructing: the unified field theory. This elusive final theory would bring quantum theory under one roof with Einstein's theory of gravity, creating a *relativistic theory of the entire field*.[373] But this Holy Grail of science remained hidden from Einstein and has yet to be uncovered. The mathematician David Hilbert, whose own theory of gravity mirrored Einstein's so closely, was already working on this unified theory in 1917. When Einstein was told of Hilbert's quest he dismissed it as *a piece of excessive boldness*, but it was eventually too tempting a prize for Einstein to resist.[374]

Eclipsing Newton
1916–1933

Einstein spent the summer and autumn of 1916 tying up the loose ends of his general theory of relativity. He also found time to revisit his 1905 paper on the quantum theory of light. His ground-breaking work on this subject would lead nearly half a century later to an invention now found in every home: the laser, used in CD players. Einstein no longer had any doubts that light quanta were a reality but he was troubled that research in this area left the *time of occurrence and direction of elementary processes to chance*.[375] It was a disturbing idea for a discipline founded on causality and predictability. In the coming years this issue would divide physics and leave Einstein isolated in the academic community. *I have the feeling that the real joke that the eternal inventor of enigmas has presented us with has not yet been absolutely understood*, Einstein told Besso in 1917.[376] Relativity and quantum theory presented differing views of the universe. Relativity was causal and explained the wave phenomena of gravitational and electromagnetic fields, whereas quantum theory showed matter to be inherently unpredictable at the atomic level and relied on probabilities to foretell events. The attempt to unify these two explanations was to occupy Einstein for many years to come.

Events in his personal life also weighed heavily on Einstein's mind. After he had pressed her for a divorce, the 41-year-old Mileva suffered a complete mental and physical collapse, followed in July 1916 by a series of heart attacks. Mileva was hospitalised and Michele Besso's wife, Anna, saw history repeating itself: first her sister Marie and now Mileva had suffered breakdowns. She added an angry postscript to a letter from her husband, but Einstein thought the comments were by Michele and defended himself: *we men are deplorable, dependent creatures, this I admit gladly to anyone. But compared to these women, every one of us is a king; for he stands more or less on his own two feet, not constantly waiting for something outside of himself to cling on to. They, however, always wait for someone to come along who will use them as he sees fit. If this doesn't happen then they simply fall to pieces.*[377] There is no doubt that Einstein was considerably less progressive in his view of women than he was in his science. But to his other friend in Zurich, Heinrich Zangger, he did admit that he was *at least partly to blame* for Mileva's *serious illness.*[378] Meanwhile Hans Albert had stopped writing to his father. Later he would tell his daughter, Evelyn, bitterly: 'Nobody has a right to expect a happy childhood.'[379] Einstein considered visiting his family, but stayed in Berlin instead and buried himself in his work: *despite my external troubles*, he wrote, *my life goes by in perfect harmony; I devote all of my thoughts to reflection.*[380]

At the beginning of 1917, Einstein himself fell ill. At first the diagnosis was gallstones, but after another collapse in the autumn the doctors decided it was a duodenal ulcer. His health was shattered: the stress of working non-stop day and night for days on end together with his erratic eating habits had taken its toll. Without Mileva to look after him he had lapsed into the lifestyle that had led to chronic digestive problems as a student. He cooked everything in a single saucepan to save time. One day Elsa's daughter, Margot, found Einstein hard-boiling an egg in a pan of soup – he hadn't even bothered to wash the eggshell, reported the horrified Margot. The doctors prescribed a strict diet and to make sure Einstein kept to it Elsa made him move in to the apartment next door. His mother, now living in southern Germany, sent food parcels as supplies were short in wartime Berlin. Einstein had lost 56 pounds during the year but now, with Elsa's help, he began to gain weight: *the food is good, and I am resting a lot* he reported.[381] But during 1918 he continued to suffer relapses, as did Mileva. To make matters worse, their son Eduard was often ill and complained of pains in his ears. When Mileva's sister, Zorka, was admitted to an asylum, Einstein feared that his younger son had inherited the mental instability of Mileva's family.

Now that they were living next door to each other, Elsa began to worry about the effect of gossip, both on her reputation and on that of her daughters. Divorce from Mileva was inevitable, although Einstein's Swiss friends continued to oppose the idea. In the summer of 1918, Mileva finally consented. As part of the settlement, Einstein agreed to give her the money from the Nobel Prize. Although he had yet to win it, he had already been nominated six times. It was a sizeable sum (about $32,000) and Mileva and the boys could live on the interest alone. The legal process was finalised on 14 February 1919, citing Einstein's adultery as grounds for divorce. The court forbade Einstein from marrying for the next two years but, never one to pay much attention to rules, he married Elsa four months later. It was a formality, as he was already living with Elsa and her daughters. Indeed, 22-year-old Ilse, who had become Einstein's paid secretary, confided to a friend that 'Albert loves me very much, perhaps more than any other man ever will' and even considered proposing to her.[382]

Einstein claimed to be *glad that my present wife understands nothing about scientific matters.*[383] Some said the vivacious and attractive Elsa was rather too keen to bask in the reflected glory of her famous husband. Hans Albert's daughter Evelyn described her as a social climber.[384] But she was also a strong and capable woman who was able to nurse Einstein through his illness and protect him from interruptions. At home she called him Albertle and together they spoke in their native dialect, liberally sprinkled with colourful sayings. Even when they emigrated to America she cooked him Swabian dishes that reminded him of the food he had eaten as a child, such as 'fried liver pasties with small egg noodles' known as *Spätzli*.[385] Like Einstein, Elsa had a mischievous sense of humour and gave a rather good impression of 'her husband in his battle with the petty side of life'.[386]

Einstein with his second wife Elsa and her daughter Margot, Berlin, 1929

Einstein was always the first to burst out laughing at these performances. It was clear to friends that she treated him as a mother would and some resented this. When Einstein sat for the painter Samuel Johnson Woolf, he described how she treated him as might 'a doting parent with a precocious child'.[387] But in truth, Einstein was happiest in such a relationship.

Physicist Philipp Frank (1884–1966) visited Einstein at Haberlandstrasse and remembered the 'beautiful furniture, carpets, and pictures', but added that 'when one entered this home, one felt that Einstein would always remain a stranger in such surroundings, a bohemian guest in a bourgeois home'.[388] In contrast, Einstein's study in the attic was spartan: bare floorboards and just one picture – an etching of Sir Isaac Newton. The shelves on one wall were packed with correspondence, typescripts, off-prints of his scientific papers, a few books and stacks of soft-covered journals. Tidying was banned and only dusting was tolerated. It was here that Einstein was sitting in early November 1919 when Elsa knocked hesitantly on his door to inform him that some journalists were waiting downstairs.

At the end of 1919, the situation in Berlin and in the rest of Germany was desperate. No buses were running because of fuel shortages and the trains had been commandeered by the military to carry emergency supplies. It was the anniversary of the Russian Revolution (1917) and the authorities feared an uprising like the Spartacist uprising in January, which had been brutally crushed and its leaders, Karl Liebknecht and Rosa Luxemburg, murdered. Roads were blocked by barbed wire and armed guards. It was not a political revolution, however, but a scientific one that astounded the world and suddenly forced Einstein into the media spotlight. The headline in *The Times* of 7 November 1919 proclaimed: REVOLUTION IN SCIENCE — NEW THEORY OF THE UNIVERSE — NEWTONIAN IDEAS OVERTHROWN.

The day before, in Britain, a joint meeting had been convened by the Royal Society and the Royal Astronomical Society at Burlington House in Piccadilly, London. There, before an audience of distinguished scientists, the results of two expeditions to Western Africa and Brazil to observe the solar eclipse were announced. In 1911, Einstein had challenged astronomers to use an eclipse to test his claim that *rays of light passing near the sun experience a deflection by its gravitational field.*[389] According to Einstein, gravity was not an instantaneous force as Newton thought, but resulted from the curvature of space-time. Large objects, such as planets, warp the geometry of space causing starlight near the sun to be bent.

Whereas once explorers had set sail to find new continents and gold, now quests were undertaken in the cause of mathematical certainty. An earlier German expedition had been thwarted by the outbreak of the Great War. When Arthur Stanley Eddington

Rosa Luxemburg (1871–1919) became a leader of the left wing of the German Social Democratic Party (SPD) in 1898. Her major theoretical work was *The Accumulation of Capital* (1912), in which she tried to prove that capitalism was doomed. In 1916 she founded the radical Spartacus League with Karl Liebknecht (1871–1919). After the Spartacist uprising in Berlin against the government, Luxemburg and Liebknecht were arrested and murdered by German soldiers in January 1919.

As seen from the earth, certain fixed stars appear to be in the neighbourhood of the sun, and are thus capable of observation during a total eclipse of the sun. At such times, these stars ought to appear to be displaced outwards from the sun by an amount indicated above, as compared with their apparent position in the sky when the sun is situated at another part of the heavens. The examination of the correctness or otherwise of this deduction is a problem of the greatest importance, the early solution of which is to be expected of astronomers. ALBERT EINSTEIN[390]

Arthur Stanley Eddington

(1882–1944), a young professor of astronomy at Cambridge, first read Einstein's paper on general relativity he described it as 'one of the most beautiful examples of the power of general mathematical reasoning'.[391] Keen to test its validity, he led the expedition to the island of Principe off the West African coast. Both expeditions faced considerable technical difficulties and in later years doubts would be raised about the accuracy of their eclipse photographs, but in November 1919 Eddington was convinced: Einstein's prediction had been triumphantly confirmed. It was a historic moment, summed up by the President of the Royal Society, Sir Joseph John Thomson (1856–1940), discoverer of the electron and winner of the Nobel Prize in 1906: ' This is the most important result obtained in connection with the theory of gravitation since Newton's day.' It was he said 'one of the highest achievements of human thought',[392] although The Times added that Thomson had to 'confess that no one had yet succeeded in stating in clear language what the theory of Einstein really was'.[393] Appropriately, the meeting took place beneath the gaze of the Royal Society's most famous president, Sir Isaac Newton, whose portrait hung on the wall. In the audience was the British philosopher and historian of science, Alfred North Whitehead (1861–1947), who described the atmosphere in the meeting as like a Greek drama. In the modern world, he said, 'the laws of physics are the decrees of fate'.[394]

Writing to Einstein in December 1919, Eddington said 'all England is talking about your theory'.[395] Not all reports were favourable, however. In a New York Times article, Charles Lane Poor, a Columbia

University astronomer, rejected Einstein's ideas as the deluded product of the 'Bolshevist' age. Relativity left him feeling as though he 'had been wandering with Alice in Wonderland and had tea with the Mad Hatter'.[396] Nevertheless, the impact of Einstein's theory on the public imagination was immense. For a generation traumatised by the Great War, Einstein offered the hope that progress was possible, that things would be different in the brave new world of tomorrow. His name became synonymous with genius and human achievement, and from this moment until his death in 1955, he was rarely out of the newspapers. His cheery round face surmounted with its untidy mop of white hair became the archetypal image of the scientist for most people, an icon of science in an uncertain world.

Bemused by this sudden fame, Einstein was bombarded with requests to explain the theory that *The Times* claimed could only be understood by twelve people in the world.[397] He thought of a typically ironic explanation a few days later. On 8 November *The Times* had referred to Einstein as a 'Swiss Jew', prompting a witty analogy: *By an application of the theory of relativity to the taste of readers, today in Germany I am called a German man of science, and in England I am represented as a Swiss Jew. If I come to be regarded as a* bête noire, *the descriptions will be reversed, and I shall become a Swiss Jew for Germans and a German man of science for the English!*[398]

Einstein's sons in Zurich were astonished to hear of their father's meteoric rise to fame. Nine-year-old Eduard asked 'Why are you so

'A wave of amazement swept over the continents. Thousands of people who had never in their lives troubled about vibrations of light and gravitation were seized by this wave and carried on high, immersed in the wish for knowledge although incapable of grasping it. This much all understood, that from the quiet study of a scholar an illuminating gospel for exploring the universe had been irradiated. During that time no name was quoted so often as that of this man. [. . .] Here was a man who had stretched his hands towards the stars; to forget earthly pains one had but to immerse oneself in his doctrine. It was the first time for ages that a chord vibrated through the world invoking all eyes towards something which, like music or religion, lay outside political or material interests.'
A Berlin journalist on Einstein[399]

AN ICON OF SCIENCE

famous, papa?', to which Einstein replied seriously: *You see, when a blind beetle crawls over the surface of a globe he doesn't notice that the track he has covered is curved. I was lucky enough to have spotted it.*[400] But as Einstein quickly realised, fame has its drawbacks. A representative of a tobacco company called at their apartment one day and asked if Einstein would permit them to use his face on a box of 'Relativity Cigars'. An insulted Einstein promptly showed him the door. *I feel now something like a whore*, he complained in a letter to Mileva. *Everybody wants to know what I am doing all the time and everybody wants to criticize.*[401]

In February 1920 Einstein's mother died. She had been ill with stomach cancer and for the last two months had stayed in Einstein's study, tended by her daughter Maja and a nurse. Einstein was deeply affected by her suffering. *One feels in one's bones the significance of blood ties*, he wrote after her death.[402] The following month he told physicist Max Born: *My father's ashes lie in Milan. I buried my mother here a few days ago. I myself have wandered continually hither and yon – a stranger everywhere. My children are in Switzerland under circumstances that make it a troublesome undertaking for me when I want to see them.*[403] The years of struggling to establish his reputation, as well as the disappointment and pain of his personal life had all taken their toll. The events of 1919 marked a turning point in Einstein's life. His greatest scientific achievements were behind him, but now as a public figure he began to take part in the political and social debates of the day.

Berliner Illustrierte Zeitung, 14 December, 1919. The picture caption reads: 'A new celebrity in world history: Albert Einstein. His research signifies a complete revolution in our concepts of nature and is on a par with the insights of Copernicus, Kepler, and Newton.'

The Weimar Republic was, to use Fritz Stern's apt phrase, a 'cauldron of resentments'.[404] Einstein had always been outspoken in his attacks on German militarism and nationalism. As a pacifist and a Jew, he became a focus of hostility among those looking for a scapegoat following Germany's defeat in the Great War and its worsening economic plight. In August 1920 a major public meeting was held at Berlin's Philharmonic Hall to inaugurate a campaign against relativity and for 'pure science'.[405] Einstein attended, a brave step for a man who admitted that *every child knows me from photographs.*[406] Anti-Semitic leaflets were handed out and Swastika lapel pins were on sale. Threatening, racist taunts were shouted at Einstein.[407]

His angry response, published on the front page of the popular *Berliner Tageblatt*, stirred up a storm of controversy. In his article, Einstein attacked leading physicist Philipp Lenard, winner of the 1905 Nobel Prize.[408] Lenard was associated with the organisers of the Berlin meeting and soon became the most high-profile critic of Einstein and relativity. At a meeting of the Society of German Natural Scientists and Physicians in September, Einstein and Lenard clashed. Relativity violated 'healthy common sense', said Lenard.[409] There was no meeting of minds and the result was a fatal polarisation of German physics. Lenard and other nationalist physicists left the meeting determined to create an Aryan physics in Germany.

It was a dangerous time to be in Berlin and Einstein considered leaving Germany as early as 1920. But he rejected Max von Laue's idea that scientists should steer clear of politics. *You see especially in the circumstances of Germany where such self-restraint leads,* wrote Einstein. *It means leaving leadership to the blind and the irresponsible, without resistance.*[410] From 1919, Einstein used his fame to campaign for humanist causes such as pacifism. Dismissed by some as naïve, it was the idealism of his vision that endeared him to thousands. According to Stern 'it was his simplicity, his otherworldliness, that impressed people. His clothes were simple, his tastes were simple, his appearance was meticulously simple. His modesty was celebrated – and genuine – as was his unselfishness. He was a lonely man, indifferent to honours, homeless by his own admission, solicitous of humanity, and diffident about his relations with those closest to him. At times he appeared like a latter-day St Francis of Assisi, a solitary saint, innocently sailing, those melancholy eyes gazing distractedly into the distance.'[411]

Zionism was one of the causes that Einstein became associated with at this time. Exposure to the widespread anti-Semitism prevalent in German society made him aware of his cultural and religious inheritance. It was in Germany, Einstein wrote, that *I discovered that I was a Jew, and this discovery was brought home to me by non-Jews rather than by Jews.*[412] He had always cherished *Jewish Ideals* such as *the pursuit of knowledge for its own sake, an almost fanatical love of justice and the desire for personal independence.*[413] The plight of the *Ostjuden*, Jewish refugees fleeing persecution in East European countries such as Poland, moved him deeply: 'An outsider all his life, in Berlin he came to identify with those individuals [. . .] who were treated as pariahs.'[414] In particular, Einstein argued that the path of assimilation chosen by his parents and fellow scientists such as Fritz Haber was wrong: *I have always been annoyed by the undignified assimilationist cravings and strivings which I have observed in so many of my friends.*[415] Einstein hoped that Zionism would revive a Jewish sense of *community* and enable Jews to *regain a dignified existence.*[416] He committed himself to the cause of founding a Hebrew University in Jerusalem, and in 1921 he agreed to accompany Chaim Weizmann (1874–1952), a biochemist and president of the World Zionist Organization, on an American fund-raising tour. He considered it his *sacred duty* to help.[417]

However, the Zionist movement knew that Einstein's support for them was limited. 'Einstein, as you know, is no Zionist,' Kurt Blumenfeld, an official of the Zionist movement, told Weizmann.[418] Although they were delighted that the great physicist was to head-

Zionism, a belief in the need to establish an autonomous Jewish home in Palestine, began with Theodor Herzl (1860–1904). A Jewish state was proclaimed in 1948 and today Zionism is supported by most Jewish communities throughout the world.

line their fund-raising tour, they were nervous about Einstein's reputation for plain speaking. Einstein had made it clear that he did not agree with Jewish nationalism any more than he did with German nationalism and he even questioned the necessity of a Jewish state in Palestine. Blumenfeld told Weizmann not to let Einstein speak at their gatherings: 'Please be very careful about this. Einstein is a bad speaker and sometimes in his naïvety will say things that are unwelcome to us.'[419]

Physicist Wolfgang Pauli once said that for Einstein there was 'no split between science and religion': 'His God is somehow involved in the immutable laws of nature. Einstein has a feeling for the central order of things. He can detect it in the simplicity of natural laws. We may take it that he felt this simplicity very strongly and directly during his discovery of the theory of relativity.'[420] Einstein was never shy of invoking the name of God to describe the sublime order of the physical world, but he did not believe in a personal God. A rabbi, who had heard that Einstein was an atheist, sent a worried telegram to him from New York: DO YOU BELIEVE IN GOD STOP PREPAID REPLY 50 WORDS. Einstein replied: *I believe in Spinoza's God who reveals himself in the harmony of all being, not in a God who concerns himself with the fate and actions of men.*[421]

Einstein and Elsa, together with Weizmann and his wife arrived in America on 1 April 1921. Much later Weizmann, who became Israel's first president, was asked whether he understood relativity. He replied dryly: 'During the journey Einstein explained his theory to me every day and on my arrival I was fully convinced that he understood it.'[422] In 1921 there were more than 50 books and pamphlets published

It seems to me that the idea of a personal God is an anthropological concept which I cannot take seriously. I feel also not able to imagine some will or goal outside the human sphere. My views are near those of Spinoza: admiration for the beauty of and belief in the logical simplicity of the order and harmony which we can grasp humbly and only imperfectly. I believe that we have to content ourselves with our imperfect knowledge and understanding and treat values and moral obligations as a purely human problem – the most important of all human problems.

ALBERT EINSTEIN, 1946[423]

SCIENCE AND GOD

on Einstein and the poet William Carlos Williams wrote a poem about him to celebrate his arrival. That year the American literary journal *The Dial* compared the Cubist revolution in the work of artists such as Pablo Picasso (1881–1973) to relativity. Every reporter wanted Einstein to explain relativity and eventually he had to sum it up in one sentence: *Time and space and gravitation have no separate existence from matter.*[424] In New York Einstein and Elsa were greeted by cheering crowds throwing streamers and flowers. *It's like the Barnum circus!* Einstein exclaimed, adding that *it must surely be more amusing to see an elephant or a giraffe than an elderly scientist.*[425] After the shortages and tensions of Berlin, the affluence of New York was overwhelming. Some 8,000 people crammed into a Manhattan hall to hear the man introduced as 'the master intellect and greatest scientist of the age'.[426] Another 3,000 waited outside hoping to catch a glimpse of him. From New York they went to Washington, then Princeton, followed by the Midwest. The last stop was Cleveland where Einstein was almost mobbed at the station by a crowd of 3,000 people.

Back in New York before departing to give his first lecture in England, Einstein wrote that he had been *exhibited like a prize ox*, but that the experience had been both exhausting and satisfying: *now it is over [. . .] there remains the beautiful feeling of having done something truly good, and of having intervened courageously on behalf of the Jewish cause, ignoring the protests of Jews and non-Jews alike.*[428] The tour was not as successful as Weizmann had hoped, but still raised $750,000. In February 1923, on a visit to Palestine, Einstein inaugurated the Hebrew University on Jerusalem's Mount Scopus (now home to more than 50,000 documents that constitute

April Einstein
through the blossomy waters
rebellious, laughing
under liberty's dead arm
has come among the daffodils
shouting
that flowers and men
were created
relatively equal.
Old-fashioned knowledge is
dead under the blossoming peach trees.

from 'St Francis Einstein of the Daffodils' (1921) by William Carlos Williams.[427]

the Einstein archive). The occasion was deeply moving, though Einstein noted in his diary that seeing fellow Jews *swaying to and fro* in prayer at the Wailing Wall was *a pathetic sight of men with a past but without a future.*[429]

In 1922 the travelling continued, with invitations to lecture in Paris and the Far East. En route to Japan in December, Einstein received the news that he had won the Nobel Prize for physics, delayed from 1921. Surprisingly he won it not for relativity but 'for his services to theoretical physics, and especially for his discovery of the law of the photoelectric effect'.[431] The delay of more than a decade in honouring Einstein was due in part to a campaign mounted by Philipp Lenard, but also because the award committee lacked theoretical physicists capable of understanding relativity. It was therefore awarded to Einstein for the tried and tested photoelectric effect. As agreed under the terms of their divorce, Einstein's prize money – 120,000 Swedish crowns (plus another 60,000 in interest) – was paid directly into a Swiss trust fund for Mileva and their sons.

After his delayed laureate's lecture to an audience of 2,000 in Göteborg on 11 July 1923, Einstein visited Danish physicist Niels Bohr in Copenhagen. The physics Nobel Prize for 1922 – announced at the same time as Einstein's – had gone to Bohr 'for his services in the investigation of the structure of atoms and of the radiation emanating from them'.[432] Einstein described Bohr's 1913 papers – which used quantum theory to explain why electrons in an atom could only occupy certain fixed orbits – as *the highest form of musicality in the sphere of thought.*[433] It seems fitting that the two most influential physicists in the 20th century were awarded the physics Nobel Prize in the same year. Indeed, according to American physicist John Wheeler, 'in

'Today, scientists no longer limit themselves to the three dimensions of Euclid. The painters have been led quite naturally, one might say by intuition, to preoccupy themselves with the new possibilities of spatial measurement which, in the language of the modern studios, are designated by the term: the fourth dimension.'

GUILLAUME APOLLINAIRE
on Cubism [430]

all the history of human thought there is no greater dialogue than that which took place over the years between Niels Bohr and Albert Einstein about the meaning of the quantum.'[434]

In September 1927 Bohr outlined his Principle of Complementarity. This description of quantum phenomena overcame what Einstein called the *dual nature of radiation*[435] – whether it is composed of waves or particles – by accepting that it is both. In order to gain a complete understanding of reality at the atomic level, physicists had

to accept that waves and particles are different but complementary views of the same phenomena. In what became known as the Copenhagen interpretation, Bohr also claimed that the experiment determines what the physicist sees. As science writer Manjit Kumar says, 'the Copenhagen interpretation suggests that observation constructs reality'.[436]

This radical and indeed paradoxical idea was compounded by Bohr's former assistant, Werner Heisenberg (1901–76). Heisenberg's Uncertainty Principle suggests that causality, a fundamental assumption of science, does not apply to the sub-atomic realm. According to Newtonian physics it should be possible to predict the course of an electron through space if we know its position and momentum. But Heisenberg pointed out that it was in fact impossible to measure both the position and the momentum of sub-atomic particles with accuracy. The more precise your measurement of the position of a particle, the greater the degree of uncertainty regarding its momentum. The uncertainty seemed to be a fundamental part of nature at

Niels Bohr

the atomic level: ' The fuzziness in knowledge is unavoidable because it is a fuzziness inherent in the universe described by these new laws of physics.'[437]

The implications of these ideas were far-reaching. Not only did they undermine the fundamental notion of causality, replacing it with a science based solely on probabilities, but they raised serious philosophical questions about the extent to which we can know the world at a sub-atomic level. Such ideas were anathema to Einstein. As early as 1920 he confessed to being irritated by this challenge to causality. He could not accept a theory that presented the physical world as inherently unpredictable. It contradicted the classical idea of an ordered and rational universe that lay at the heart of Einstein's physics. As he said in a letter to Max Born, the principle architect of the new quantum mechanics: *The theory yields much, but it hardly brings us closer to the Old One's secrets. I, in any case, am convinced that He does not play dice.*[438] For Einstein, causality was not a concept that was limited to the world of our everyday experiences: *Like the moon has a definite position whether or not we look at the moon, the same must also hold for atomic objects, as there is no sharp distinction possible between these and macroscopic objects.*[439] The theories of the Copenhagen interpretation were, for Einstein, *a temporary expedient.*[440] He argued that we simply lacked the right theoretical understanding, a situation that his unified field theory would rectify.

Einstein had agreed to present a paper at the Fifth Solvay Congress in October 1927 on the current state of research in quantum mechanics. In the end he decided not to do so, but during the conference Einstein and Bohr engaged in an intense debate about quantum theory. It was a turning point in Einstein's career. Although quantum theory had been a central concern of his early work, he disagreed strongly with the way in which younger physicists such as Heisenberg and Pauli approached the problem.

According to Heisenberg, the debate between Einstein and Bohr was largely conducted outside the conference room. The titanic clash of minds would begin over breakfast. Einstein would propose a thought experiment to Bohr who would spend the day discussing it with his colleagues before returning with a solution. 'Einstein would look a bit worried,' reports Heisenberg, 'but by next morning he was ready with a new imaginary experiment more complicated than the last, and this time, so he avowed, bound to invalidate the uncertainty principle. This attempt would fare no better by evening, and after the same game had been continued for a few days, Einstein's friend Paul Ehrenfest [. . .] said: "Einstein, I am ashamed of you; you are arguing against the new quantum theory just as your opponents argue about relativity theory." But even this friendly admonition went unheard. Once again it was driven home to me how terribly difficult it is to give up an attitude on which one's entire scientific approach and career have been based. [. . .] Einstein was not pre-pared to let us do what, to him, amounted to pulling the ground from under his feet. [. . .] *God does not throw dice* was his unshakable principle, one that he would not allow anybody to challenge. To which Bohr could only counter with: "Nor is it our business to prescribe to God how He should run the world."'[441]

After 1927 Einstein concentrated his efforts on developing a theory that would bring quantum theory into the mainstream of physics. His search for a unified field theory was to remain unfinished at his death, although in recent years physicists have again taken up this quest. String theory is one such attempt to unify the forces of nature into a theory of everything. At the end of his life Einstein confessed to a friend that 50 long years of *conscious brooding* about quantum theory had been in vain.[442] Max Born, who thought that even with-out relativity Einstein would be 'one of the greatest theoretical physi-cists of all time', expressed regret that Einstein turned his back on the new physics that he had helped found: 'Many of us regard this as a tragedy – for him, as he gropes his way in loneliness, and for us, who miss our leader and standard-bearer.'[443]

In 1928 Einstein collapsed while lecturing in Switzerland. His doctor diagnosed acute dilation of the heart brought about by extreme physical exertion (Einstein had been carrying his luggage through deep snow). Back in Berlin he was put on a salt-free diet, banned from smoking, and confined to bed. Afterwards he admitted: *I was close to croaking, which of course one shouldn't put off unduly.*[444] Even so, during his convalescence Einstein continued to work on his unified theory, on one occasion covering his bed sheets with equations. It was, he said, a *marvellous theory* and his results were *beautiful*,[445] but when it was published in 1929 younger physicists such as Pauli knew that it was only a partial solution.

After Einstein's collapse Elsa decided she could not run the home, nurse him and take care of his ever increasing correspondence. So 32-year-old Helen Dukas, who came from Elsa's birthplace of Hechingen in Swabia, became Einstein's secretary. Helen soon became indispensable to Einstein and remained with him until his death. When Elsa died, she took over the running of the household as well. A previous secretary, Betty Neumann, had become his lover. Einstein had met this attractive 23-year-old in 1923 while she was visiting from Austria. He arranged for her to work as his secretary at the physics institute where he saw her two days a week, with Elsa's tacit approval. The affair came to an end in 1924 and Einstein wrote that he would have to 'seek in the stars what was denied him on earth'.[446]

In the so-called Golden Twenties, Einstein was an attractive man whose social circle included some of the most influential people in Europe. One visitor's first impression of him was of 'stunning youthfulness, very romantic and at certain moments irresistibly reminiscent of the young Beethoven'.[447] During these years there were other affairs, with Margarete Lenbach and Estella Katzenellenbogen for instance, although he was careful to cover his tracks, asking them to destroy his correspondence. Although Einstein wrote of *the hard test of patience which marriage invariably involves* it is clear that Elsa's experience was no less trying.[448] 'But,' she wrote, 'the Lord has put into him so much that's beautiful, and I find him wonderful, even though life at his side is enervating and difficult [. . .] in every respect.'[449]

Einstein's 50th birthday in 1929 brought congratulatory tele-grams from the German chancellor, the king of Spain, the Japanese emperor, and Herbert Hoover, the president of the United States. However, Einstein was most impressed by the gift of a small pouch of pipe tobacco from an unemployed man. In a note the man made a witty allusion to both relativity and field theory: 'There is relatively little tobacco, but it is from a good field.'[450]

Einstein's students and a bank had clubbed together to buy him a sailing boat and that summer the Einsteins commissioned an archi-tect to build them a summer home at Caputh, just south of Potsdam near the Lakes Templin and Schwielow. The house, built entirely of wood, was designed by Konrad Wachsmann according to Bauhaus principles, with furniture commissioned from the Bauhaus architect Marcel Breuer. The revolutionary prefabricated building took just 14 days to construct. Elsa described the four-bedroom house as 'very artistic, very modern'.[451] According to family friend Antonina Vallentin, the Landhaus Einstein was 'as simple as a mathematical formula'.[452] Best of all, as far as Einstein was concerned, it was just three minutes' walk from the water.

Sailing was Einstein's main form of relaxation after playing the violin. As his fame increased, sailing allowed him to escape from the clamour of the modern world. Vallentin once described a trip on his boat: 'Wearing sandals and an old sweater, his hair ruffling in the breeze, he would stand upright rocking gently with the motion of the boat, completely at one with the sail he was manoeuvring. [. . .] At such moments he looked like anything in the world except a scientist. He was absurdly happy as soon as he reached the water.'[453] However, Einstein was not the world's most competent sailor. His

The Bauhaus was the most famous school of architecture and design of the 20th century. Founded in 1919 by German architect Walter Gropius (1883–1969), its teachers included the painters Paul Klee (1879–1940) and Wassily Kandinsky (1866–1944). It moved from Weimar to Dessau and was closed by the Nazis in 1933.

elder son, Hans Albert, now a 25-year-old engineer, was one of the first to be taken out on Einstein's new boat, the *Tümmler* (meaning 'Porpoise'), and recalls that his father almost crashed it on the rocky shoreline. On another visit Einstein advised his son: *don't have any children: it makes divorce so much more complicated*.[454] Hans Albert ignored this advice and his wife Frieda gave birth to a son, Bernhard Caesar, in 1930.

Einstein's relationship with his younger son, Eduard, broke down in 1930. A sickly but precociously gifted child (he was reading Goethe and Schiller at the age of nine), Eduard inherited his father's interest in music. Vallentin once heard him playing on his father's piano at Haberlandstrasse, and noticed that his 'faraway expression' was 'irreparably sad'.[455] Eduard Einstein idolised his father, but he never forgave him for deserting the family when he was only four. In 1930 he suffered a mental breakdown and sent Einstein a series of incoherent, hate-filled letters. His condition worsened throughout the 1930s and when he eventually became violent Mileva reluctantly agreed that he should be committed to a psychiatric hospital. His son's breakdown only confirmed Einstein's deep fear of mental instability. As his second wife, Elsa, reported: 'This sorrow is eating up Albert. He finds it difficult to cope with it, more difficult than he would care to admit. He has always aimed at being invulnerable to everything that concerned him personally. He really is so, much more than any other man I know. But this has hit him very hard.'[456] Eduard never recovered from his schizophrenia and Mileva devoted the rest of her life to caring for him. He died in 1965.

The Wall Street Crash of October 1929 delivered a *coup de grâce* to the fragile economy and political order of the Weimar Republic. In the next three years bankruptcies and unemployment increased dramatically. In the September 1930 elections, Adolf Hitler's National Socialists capitalised on public dissatisfaction and became the second largest party in the Reichstag. As the economic conditions steadily worsened, it was in the streets rather than parliament that the battle for political dominance was fought. There were frequent clashes between the communists and the fascists in Berlin.

Long before the infamous *Kristallnacht* on 9 November 1938, when synagogues were systematically burnt and Jewish property looted, anti-Semitism represented a real danger to Einstein, who had joked in 1926 that he had become a *Jewish saint*.[457] A right-wing student threatened to cut his throat during one of his lectures, after Berlin anti-Semite Rudolph Leibus offered a reward to anyone who killed Einstein. Even after the September 1930 elections, Einstein mistakenly saw the Nazis as a *childish disease of the Republic* that would soon pass.[458] Despite the oppressive atmosphere of anti-Semitism, he wanted to stay in Berlin, which Heisenberg described as 'the stronghold of physics in Germany'.[459]

There was no shortage of offers from foreign universities, however. In December 1930 Einstein began a visiting professorship at the California Institute of Technology (Caltech) in Pasadena, USA, where he worked with Edwin Hubble, the astronomer who had recently demonstrated that Einstein's cosmological constant was wrong. When he returned to Germany in March, Einstein spent most of his time working at his new home in Caputh, away from the political hothouse of Berlin. In May 1931 he delivered a lecture at the University of Oxford and was offered a prestigious research fellowship at Christ Church College. This enabled him to divide his working year between Britain and America, and as a result he was rarely seen in Germany.

It was at Oxford in spring 1932 that Einstein first met the American educationalist Abraham Flexner (1866–1959). Flexner was in Europe head-hunting for a new institute of advanced study, to be located on the east coast of America at Princeton, where scholars could concentrate on research without troubling themselves with the mundane paperwork Einstein had always hated. In May Flexner visited Einstein at Caputh, but the physicist was not yet ready to leave Germany. After long discussions, however, he agreed to spend half the year working in Princeton, beginning in autumn 1933. After Flexner had left, Antonina Vallentin visited the Einsteins. She had been warned by the commander in chief of the German army, General von Seeckt, that Einstein's life was in danger. Appalled by the atmosphere of violence and intimidation in Germany, Vallentin tried desperately to convince Einstein to emigrate. Elsa confided in her that she 'would like him to keep silent for the moment, not sign any manifestos, and devote himself solely to his own problems'.[460]

In December 1932 they prepared to depart for their winter visit to Caltech in Pasadena. Einstein informed his colleagues at the University of Berlin that he would return the following April, but privately he was not sure. *Take a good look at it,* Einstein said to Elsa as they left their house in Caputh. *You will never see it again.*[461]

Events proved him right. In January 1933 Hitler became Chancellor. A month later the Reichstag was torched, which the Nazis used as an excuse to suspend most civil liberties. In March 1933 the first concentration camp was opened at Dachau near Munich. In that same month, Nazi storm-troopers searched Einstein's beloved home at Caputh. They found nothing – Margot had secretly arranged for his papers to be transferred to the French embassy in Berlin before escaping to Paris. In spring, Jews began to be excluded from the civil service and academia. Then, in Berlin on 10 May, Hitler's Minister of Propaganda, Joseph Goebbels, presided over the public burning of books by Jewish and socialist intellectuals, including the playwright Bertholt Brecht (1898–1956) and Sigmund Freud (1856–1939), pioneer of psychoanalysis. Soon even school maths lessons were polluted by nationalist propaganda, students having to calculate the distance covered in certain times by tanks and torpedo boats. A terrible new era had dawned in Germany and Einstein had escaped just in time.

The Struggle for Truth
1933—1955

For Einstein, the 1930s were to be a decade of new beginnings but also sad farewells. From his new home in Princeton he watched with alarm as the cancer of fascism spread throughout Europe. Controversially, Flexner tried to prevent his new employee at the Institute for Advanced Study from speaking out on political issues. 'Your safety in America depends upon your silence and refraining from attendance at public functions,' he told Einstein, anxious to avoid offending his conservative benefactors.[462] Einstein refused to be muzzled, but he was more careful about his public statements. Behind the scenes, however, he worked tirelessly to help Jews fleeing persecution in Europe, not just in Germany but also in the Soviet Union. Following the trial of the Jewish revolutionary Leon Trotsky (1879–1940), Einstein wrote to the Russian dictator Joseph Stalin (1879–1953) in 1936 to ask for clemency. His pleas were unsuccessful, but for others, such as violinist Boris Schwarz, with whom Einstein had played in the 1920s, the physicist's intervention meant a ticket out of Nazi Germany and escape from certain death.

Before he settled in Princeton, Einstein returned briefly to Europe at the end of March 1933. On the ship Einstein reluctantly decided to resign from the Prussian Academy. In his letter he referred to the *beautiful personal relations* he had enjoyed in the Academy of Sciences.[463] Einstein was less sorry about renouncing his German citizenship, which he did immediately on arrival in Belgium. He would never again enter the land of his birth. The Nazi press was jubilant. GOOD NEWS OF EINSTEIN – HE IS NOT COMING BACK!

boasted one.[464] For Lenard and other nationalist physicists it was time to reject 'Jewish physics' and to create a new Aryan science.[465] But Max Planck, whose son Erwin was executed by the Nazis in 1945 for his part in a plot against Hitler, knew that it was Germany's loss. 'Even though in political matters a deep gulf divides us,' he said, 'I am also absolutely certain that in the centuries to come Einstein will be celebrated as one of the brightest stars that has ever shone on our Academy.'[466] Nevertheless, when Hitler ordered the purging of Jewish academics from the universities, Planck declined to join a protest organised by colleagues such as chemist Otto Hahn. At least 25 per cent of lecturers holding a post in 1933 were forced out and it spelled disaster for German science. Soon even Einstein's name was banned from physics departments, a situation depicted in Brecht's play *Fear and Misery in the Third Reich* (1935–8), which was written in exile. With a bounty of $5,000 on his head (*I didn't know I was worth that much!* he joked)[467] and his property confiscated by the German state, Einstein knew his future lay in America. Before leaving Europe, however, he visited Switzerland where he met Mileva and Eduard for the last time.

Einstein departed for America from Southampton on 7 October 1933. In England he had ignored Flexner's protests and addressed 10,000 people in the Royal Albert Hall in the cause of exiled German scientists. The police had received a tip-off that an attempt might be made to assassinate him and security was tight. Einstein praised the British people for remaining *faithful to the tradition of tolerance and justice* and looked forward to a better future. *Let us hope that, at some future time, when Europe is politically and economically united, the historian rendering judgement will be able to say that, in our own days, the liberty and honour of this continent were saved by the nations of Western Europe; that they stood fast in bitter times against the forces of hatred and oppression; that they successfully defended that which has brought us every advance in knowledge and invention: the freedom of the individual without which no self-respecting individual finds life worth living.*[468]

Einstein was 'the acknowledged international champion of pacifism' at the beginning of the 1930s, according to the physicist Joseph Rotblat (*b*.1908), who won the Nobel Peace Prize in 1995.[469] But when Einstein advised a Belgian conscientious objector in 1933 to enlist and help *save European civilization*,[470] he became for some 'an apostate, a traitor to the cause of peace'.[471] Einstein was convinced, however, that *should German armed might prevail, life will not be worth living anywhere in Europe.*[472] Before boarding the ship bound for New York, he conveyed his fears about German militarism to Winston Churchill (1874–1965) and David Lloyd George (1863–1945).

Although Einstein found a safe haven in America, he remained a controversial figure. On the other side of the Atlantic many were attracted to fascism and 'sizable crowds of Americans were enthusiastic and vociferous supporters' of Hitler.[473] Mrs James Gray of the Woman's Patriot Corporation even attempted to prevent Einstein from entering America, claiming 'He's a radical and an alien Red!'[474]

Einstein and Helen Dukas, Princeton, 1940

In response Einstein described himself as *one who is wicked enough to reject every kind of war, except the inexorable war with one's own spouse.*[475] Nevertheless, Princeton was proud of its new resident. Science writer Ed Regis describes how overnight 'Princeton was transformed from a gentleman's college town into a world centre for physics.'[476] As physicist Paul Langevin (1872–1946) put it, 'the Pope of Physics has moved.'[477]

On his first visit to the town in 1921, Einstein had compared Princeton to *an as yet unsmoked pipe, so fresh, so young.*[478] In October 1933, the Einsteins and Helen Dukas rented a house at 2 Library Place. There was a musical house-warming party, with Einstein playing second fiddle in a string quartet. They moved again in autumn 1935 to nearby 112 Mercer Street, the last of Einstein's many homes. He paid for it in cash with money raised from the sale of a 1912 manuscript on relativity to the Morgan Library in New York.

The Einsteins immediately felt at home in Princeton. Einstein told his sister that his greatest pleasure was sailing on the Connecticut River: *in over-populated Europe one can hardly imagine such wild, unspoiled nature.*[479] Elsa said 'the whole of Princeton is one great park with wonderful trees'. It reminded her of living in Oxford in 'the heart of England'.[480] Einstein was less flattering, however, about the university town's academics whom he described as *puny demigods on stilts.*[481]

Initially the Institute for Advanced Study did not have its own quarters and Einstein had an office in Fine Hall, the mathematics department at Princeton University. To this day a remark Einstein made on his first visit in 1921 is inscribed above the fireplace in the faculty lounge: *Raffiniert ist der Herr Gott, aber boshaft ist Er nicht – Subtle is the Lord, but malicious He is not.*[482] Among his new colleagues were the brilliant mathematicians John von Neumann (1903–57) and Kurt Gödel (1906–78). Einstein's only duty apart from research was to attend occasional faculty meetings. In 1934 his original contract

Einstein sailing with Elsa, 1934

to teach for five months of the year was converted to a full professorship, with a salary double that of most Princeton professors.

In the next two decades, Einstein left America only once, sailing to Bermuda in 1935 to make an application for an immigrant visa, which could be filed only at a foreign consulate. He and Elsa had decided to make America their home, a process that was completed on 22 June 1940 when Einstein was sworn in as a citizen of the United States. Sadly Elsa did not live long enough to take the oath. In the summer of 1934 her daughter, Ilse, died from cancer and not long afterwards Elsa, too, fell ill. A disorder of the heart and kidneys was diagnosed. She was cared for by her daughter, Margot, and Helen Dukas, who gradually took over the running of Einstein's home as well as his office. In the winter of 1936, Elsa's illness worsened and she was confined to her bed. Einstein sat beside her for many hours, reading and talking to the woman with whom he had spent almost two decades of his life. Elsa died on 20 December 1936. Einstein was 'utterly ashen and shaken', but when it was suggested he take a break from his work he replied: *No, now more than ever I need to work. I have to go on.*[483]

The year that saw the start of the Spanish Civil War had brought Einstein nothing but bad news. His friend Marcel Grossmann had died earlier in 1936 and, in an emotional letter to his widow, Einstein remembered their time as students in Zurich: *our conversations over iced coffee in the Metropole every few weeks are among my happiest memories.* He contrasted his *beautiful* friendship with Marcel with his *inwardly solitary* situation now.[484] That same year two young women had independently claimed to be Einstein's illegitimate daughter. He was sufficiently concerned about one to hire an investigator to look into her background, but both turned out to be bogus.

Just before Elsa's death Einstein had told his sister how *as in my youth, I sit here endlessly and think and calculate, hoping to unearth deep secrets. The so-called Great World, i.e. men's bustle, has less attraction than ever, so that each day I find myself becoming more of a hermit.*[485] Now without his wife – who had been *more attached to other people than I am*[486] – Einstein redoubled his efforts to discover the unified field theory.

Princeton provided a genteel and peaceful haven in which to pursue his science, protected from intrusive journalists by the formidable Helen Dukas. However, a neighbour's daughter did manage to slip past Dukas, looking for help with her maths homework. When her parents apologised to the great physicist he replied: *That's quite unnecessary. I'm learning just as much from your child as she is learning from me.*[487] Einstein's friends at Princeton were not from the academic establishment but were mostly outsiders like himself, exiles from Europe such as the philosopher Oppenheim, historian Erich von Kahler (1885–1970), or the novelist and mathematician Hermann Broch (1886–1951), whom Einstein had helped escape from Austria. Novelist Thomas Mann also fled Nazi Germany, arriving in Princeton in 1938.

In 1937 Einstein helped a colleague, Leopold Infeld (1898–1968), whose fellowship at the Institute had expired, to earn enough money to stay in Princeton by collaborating with him on a popular history of science: *The Evolution of Physics* (1938). Infeld described Einstein at this time as grey-haired, 'his face tired and yellow', but with the 'same radiant deep eyes' as when he had first met him in Berlin.[488] He wore an old brown leather jacket and shoes without socks. In *The Evolution of Physics* Einstein and Infeld found a memorable analogy for the physicist's difficult task: *In our endeavour to understand reality we are somewhat like a man trying to understand the mechanism of a closed watch. He sees the face and the moving hands, even hears its ticking, but he has no way of opening the case. If he is ingenious he may form some picture of a mechanism which could be responsible for all the things he observes, but he may never be quite sure his picture is the only one which could explain his observations.*[489] Einstein and Infeld depict the physicist as a modern Sherlock Holmes, using *pure thinking* to piece together the *strange, incoherent, and wholly unrelated* facts of the case. *So he plays his violin, or lounges in his armchair enjoying a pipe, when suddenly, by Jove, he has it!*[490] Of course this detective is none other than Einstein himself, with his trademark pipe and violin. But for Einstein in the 1930s there was no Eureka moment. The book of nature, which according to Galileo was written in the language of mathematics, refused to add up.

When his close friend Paul Ehrenfest committed suicide in September 1933, Einstein wrote of the *increasing difficulty of adaption to new ideas which always confronts the man past fifty*.[491] As he ploughed a lonely furrow in his work on the elusive unified field theory, younger scientists were busy applying his earlier work on both quantum theory and relativity to nuclear physics. Their research would lead ultimately to the atomic bomb. During the 1930s Einstein did not follow events in nuclear physics closely. His gaze was directed elsewhere, to achieving the ultimate theoretical synthesis that would bring the laws governing atomic particles into line with those that rule the stars and the planets. He also continued to find fault with the work of the quantum theorists, such as in his 1935 paper on what became known as the Einstein-Podolsky-Rosen paradox. Einstein argued that the description of reality provided by Heisenberg's Uncertainty Principle was incomplete, thereby justifying his own continued search for the unified field theory.

Despite Einstein's theoretical reservations, quantum theory was being used successfully to describe nuclear reactions. Using neutrons (an electrically neutral particle), scientists bombarded heavy uranium atoms, attempting to split them into the lighter elements, boron and krypton. The Italian nuclear physicist Enrico Fermi (1901–54) first attempted this in Rome in 1935 using slow neutrons to produce new radioactive elements (for which he won the Nobel Prize in 1938). But the real breakthrough came just before Christmas that year. Working in Berlin, Otto Hahn and Fritz Strassmann (1902–80) could not understand why bombarding uranium with neutrons appeared to yield barium, an element that is just over half as heavy and which carries a little over half the charge of uranium. They turned to their former colleague Lise Meitner (1878–1968) for help. Meitner, who had been forced to leave Germany because she was Jewish, replied that although their results were astonishing, it was not inconceivable that the heavy and unstable uranium atom had actually split in two. Meitner's nephew, Otto Frisch (1904–79), who was working in Copenhagen at Niels Bohr's Institute for Theoretical Physics, used a cloud chamber to confirm this. It was Frisch who first described the splitting of the atom using a term from biology for the division of a bacterium: 'fission'. As the historian of the atomic bomb Richard Rhodes has said, 'thereby the name for a multiplication of life became the name for a violent process of destruction'.[492]

It was Leo Szilard – a brilliant Hungarian physicist with whom Einstein had once patented a refrigerator – who realised that the key to liberating the energy locked inside the atom lay in creating a self-sustaining chain reaction. In 1938, both Fermi and Szilard were in America when news reached them of Hahn and Strassmann's experiment. Szilard immediately realised that nuclear weapons were now a reality. Einstein had ruled out *a shattering of the atom* in 1919, in discussion with Berlin journalist, Alexander Moszkowski, insisting that *science in its present state makes it appear almost impossible that we shall ever succeed in so doing.*[493] Even in 1934 he denied that an atomic bomb was possible: *Splitting the atom by bombardment is like shooting at birds in the dark in a region where there are few birds.*[494] But in July 1939, Szilard knocked on Einstein's door with the news that a chain reaction was now possible. Einstein was shocked. *Daran habe ich gar nicht gedacht!* was his reaction – *I never thought of that!*[495]

Together they wrote a fateful letter to President Roosevelt. This letter, signed by Einstein, warned *that extremely powerful bombs of a new type* were now possible. *A single bomb of this type, carried by boat or exploded in a port might very well destroy the whole port together with some of the surrounding territory.*[496] Einstein advised that the United States should secure for itself a supply of uranium and press ahead with experimental research into this new lethal science before Germany could gain the upper hand. In Europe events were moving fast.

On 1 September Germany launched its *Blitzkrieg* against Poland and within days Britain and France were at war with Hitler. When Roosevelt finally read the letter on 11 October he saw the threat immediately: 'This requires action,' he said.[497] That same evening the Advisory Committee on Uranium was convened to investigate the military applications of fission.

The building of the atomic bomb, code-named the Manhattan Project, was the largest and most expensive scientific project ever undertaken. Ironically, many of the physicists were exiles from Hitler's Germany. The bomb that exploded above the city of Hiroshima on 6 August 1945 produced temperatures on the ground of 3,000–4,000°C and killed 100,000 people instantly. Three days later more than 70,000 people were killed at Nagasaki. These appalling death tolls doubled in the coming years as a result of lethal radiation.

Einstein played no part in developing the atomic bomb, as his radical views meant he was seen as a security risk. After the war he admitted that signing the letter to Roosevelt was the *one mistake in my life*.[498] As it turned out, his fear that the Nazis would soon have a bomb proved unfounded as Hitler's racist policies had stripped Germany of its best scientists. Many of Einstein's relatives were murdered by the Nazis, including two cousins who died in Auschwitz and Theresienstadt. After the war, Otto Hahn's request that he become an honourary member of the newly founded Max Planck Society met with a blunt response from Einstein: *The crimes of the Germans are really the most hideous that the history of the so-called civilized nations has to show. The attitude of the German intellectuals – viewed as a class – was no better than that of the mob.*[499] He even prevented German publishers from reprinting his 1916 popularisation of relativity. Although he remained close to individuals such as Laue and Planck (who died in 1947), Einstein had finally cut himself free from the land of his birth.

Atomic power was *no more unnatural than when I sail a boat on Saranac Lake*, Einstein insisted,[500] but in the post-war period he took it upon

in the United States became incriminating evidence. These documents are a chilling reminder of Cold War paranoia, but they also provide an amusing insight into the strange mixture of half-truths and malicious gossip that secret services feed on. One especially silly memo cites the *Arlington Daily* from 21 May 1948 as reporting that Professor Einstein attended a secret meeting with 'ten former Nazi research brain-trusters' at which they put on asbestos suits and watched while a beam of light was used to melt a block of metal. The atomic bomb was 'little boy stuff' compared to this new weapon which could destroy entire cities.[506] Einstein had no idea that his life and politics were being so closely monitored by the FBI.

Later, J Edgar Hoover's suspicions shifted to Einstein's secretary, but an FBI interview with Dukas in September 1951 proved inconclusive. Hoover never plucked up the courage to interview Einstein himself, but he would surely have done so had he known that Einstein had a love affair with a Soviet spy during the Second World War. Her name was Margarita Konenkova, wife of the sculptor Sergei Konenkov, who made a fine bronze bust of Einstein in 1935. Margarita's mission was to introduce Einstein to the Soviet vice-consul in New York, which she did, but there is no evidence that Einstein knew she was a spy. In their love letters, written when Margarita had returned to Moscow in 1945, Einstein refers to his Princeton home as his *hermit's cell* or his *lonely nest*.[507] In another he talks of his failing health with typical humour: *I'm happy, now that I've finally escaped the tender claws of medicine and have seen the Nest again, which sends you its best greetings. Half my time is taken up with medical procedures. Today, I had two of my teeth pulled, so that a fearsome bit of machinery could be fitted in my mouth. When that's all done, I'll truly be an American.*[508]

Of course, Einstein was neither a spy nor a communist. In 1933 he wrote *I am an adversary of Bolshevism just as much as of Fascism. I am against all dictatorships.*[509] In the 1950s he became seriously concerned by what he saw as the rise of fascist forces in America arguing for civil liberties to be curtailed. In January 1953 Einstein wrote to President Harry

S Truman on behalf of the atomic spies Julius and Ethel Rosenberg, but his pleas fell on deaf ears and they were executed six months later. The infamous Senator Joseph McCarthy (1908–57) even described Einstein as an 'enemy of America',[510] but others just said Einstein was naïve about politics. John Stachel, who has edited Einstein's collected papers, disagrees, praising his ability to cut through 'inextricable complications to what he saw as the heart of the matter'.[511]

After the war Einstein's health noticeably declined. In 1947 he joked to quantum physicist Erwin Schrödinger (1887–1961) that he had become so weak that he *looked like a spectre*.[512] In December 1948, he was admitted to the Jewish Hospital in Brooklyn suffering abdominal pains and vomiting. An ulcer was suspected, but a surgeon discovered an aneurysm, a balloon-like swelling of the aorta, the main artery in the abdomen. It was the size of a grapefruit and the doctors knew that a fatal perforation was only a matter of time. Einstein's father had died of heart disease and the usual cause of this kind of aneurysm is atherosclerosis or clogging of the arteries

Ethel Rosenberg (née Greenglass, 1915–53) was a clerk for a shipping company until she was sacked for organising a strike by 150 women workers. She joined the Young Communist League and became a member of the American Communist Party. In 1939 she married Julius Rosenberg (1918–53), chairman of the Party's Industrial Division, and they held meetings at their apartment. Julius was an inspector at the US Army Signal Corps until 1945 when his membership of the Party came to light. In 1950 Ethel's brother accused Julius of being in a spy ring. The Rosenbergs were arrested, found guilty of espionage, and executed.

by fatty deposits. Einstein left hospital a month later. Later he thanked the surgeon, Rudolph Nissen, sending him a photo clipped from a newspaper in which he stuck out his tongue at journalists. On it he wrote: *To Nissen my tummy / the world my tongue!* [513]

On 4 August 1948 Mileva died in Zurich, after suffering a stroke that had partially paralysed her. Before her death, a dispute over the ownership of her home had caused Einstein and his ex-wife to lapse once again into mutual animosity. In July 1947 he wrote: *When the house has been sold and Tetel* [Eduard] *has a reliable guardian, and Mileva is no longer with us, I will be able to go to my grave with peace of mind.* [514] Mileva's fatal stroke occurred after their schizophrenic son, Eduard, ransacked her apartment looking for an object that existed only in his mind. A friend said 'She died alone. She died quite alone.' [515]

Einstein had no contact with Eduard in his later years, a silence that was *based on an inhibition that I am not fully capable of analyzing.* [516] Carl Seelig visited Eduard Einstein at an asylum in 1952 and reported: 'The face of your son has something tormented and brooding, but also a serene smile and a trustfulness that are speedily charming.' [517] Einstein was close to neither of his sons and rarely met Hans Albert who had emigrated to America in 1937. For Hans Albert's 50th birthday in 1954, Einstein complimented him on having inherited *the main traits of my personality: the ability to rise above mere existence by sacrificing one's self through the years for an impersonal goal. This is the best, indeed the only thing through which we can make ourselves independent from personal fate and other human beings.* [518] Much later, Hans Albert said that Einstein could never remember his birthday and had to be reminded it was his fiftieth.

Einstein's own 70th birthday celebrations found the physicist uncharacteristically depressed and isolated. His health was failing, as was that of his sister, Maja, who had lived in Florence until 1939, when Mussolini's anti-Semitic policies forced her to join her brother in Princeton. In 1946, Maja had suffered a stroke from which she never recovered. She was nursed by Margot at their Princeton home, and Einstein read to her every evening, as he had to Elsa during her illness. When Maja died on 25 June 1951 he wrote *I miss her more than can be imagined.*[519]

One final honour awaited the man who once described himself as a *Jewish saint*: the presidency of Israel. Weizmann had been Israel's first president, but when he died in 1952, Israel's prime minister, David Ben-Gurion (1886–1973), felt obliged to offer the presidency to 'the greatest Jew on earth'.[520] Although Einstein welcomed the founding of the state of Israel in 1948, as late as 1946 he had upset Zionists by calling for Palestine to be governed by an international body. Ben-Gurion knew the physicist's irascible character would make life difficult: 'if he accepts we are in for trouble', he said privately.[521] But Einstein was rather embarrassed by the honour and gracefully declined: *I am deeply moved by the offer from our state Israel, and at once saddened and ashamed that I cannot accept it. All my life I have dealt with objective matters, hence I lack both the natural aptitude and the experience to deal properly with people and to exercise official functions. For these reasons alone I would be unsuited to fulfil the duties of that high office, even if advancing age was not making increasing demands on my strength.*[522] He told Margot that if he became president he would have no choice but to tell the Israeli people things they did not want to hear.

On Einstein's 74th birthday in 1953 a card arrived addressed 'To the President of the Olympia Academy, Albert Einstein, Princeton, New Jersey, USA.' It was from his old friends Habicht and Solovine who had met in Paris two days earlier. Their happy memories of evenings spent discussing physics and philosophy in Bern half a century ago moved them to write to their former mentor and friend: 'To the Right Reverend, incomparable President of our Academy: In your non-presence, despite the reserved seat, there was held today a sad-solemn session of our world-famous Academy. The reserved seat, which we always keep warm, *awaits*, yes, *awaits* and *awaits* your coming. – Habicht.

'I also, erstwhile member of the glorious Academy, have great difficulty holding back my tears when I see the empty chair that you should have occupied. There remains for me only to convey to you my most humble, most reverent, and heartfelt greetings. – M Solovine.'[523]

Einstein was deeply moved by this touching personal tribute from friends separated from him by so many miles and half a lifetime. His reply is full of nostalgia but also humour: *In your short life, dear Academy, you took delight, with childlike joy, in all that was clear and intelligent. Your members created you to make fun of your long-established sister Academies.* But, he concluded, its *bright, vivifying radiance still lights our lonely pilgrimage.*[524]

Although he had retired officially in 1946, Einstein worked until the very end on his Holy Grail, the unified field theory. It remained tantalisingly out of reach: *I feel like a kid who can't get the hang of the ABCs,* he wrote, *even though, strangely enough, I still don't abandon hope. After all, one is dealing here with a sphinx, not with a willing streetwalker.*[525] In what were to be his last words on science, he spoke of the intransigence of the problems that faced him: *It appears doubtful that a [classical] field theory can account for the atomistic structure of matter and radiation as well as of quantum phenomena. Most physicists will reply with a firm 'no', since they believe that the quantum problem has been solved in principle by other means. However that may be, Lessing's comforting words stay with us: 'The struggle for truth is more precious than its assured possession.'*[526]

Back in 1897 he had told Pauline Winteler that intellectual work and the study of nature were the *relentlessly strict angels* that would guide him through life. True to his word, Einstein had dedicated himself to the *struggle for truth.* In the same month as he wrote these words, he learnt that his closest friend, Michele Besso, had died aged 82. Shortly before his own death, Einstein wrote a moving letter to Besso's son. What he had admired most in Besso, he said, *was the fact that he managed for many years to live with his wife not only in peace but in continuing harmony – an undertaking in which rather shamefully I failed twice.*[527] As a young man Einstein had criticised Besso's unwillingness to commit himself body and soul to scientific research; he was, said Einstein, a perpetual student and an *awful schlemiel.*[528] But now

Einstein's words of admiration for his friend were poignant and heartfelt. At the end of his life, Einstein realised that the struggle for truth had exacted a heavy price in his personal life.

On Wednesday 13 April 1955 Einstein collapsed at home; the aneurysm had ruptured. Although he knew he was dying, he refused surgery: *I want to go when I want,* he said. *It is tasteless to prolong life artificially; I have done my share, it is time to go. I will do it elegantly.*[529] On Friday he had to be moved to Princeton hospital, and his son Hans Albert was called. By Sunday Einstein was asking for a pen and paper to continue working, but early the following morning a nurse noticed he was having difficulty breathing. As she raised the head of the bed, at 1.10 a.m., Einstein mumbled some words in German and died. An autopsy was carried out the same morning, Monday 18 April, by Dr Thomas F Harvey who confirmed that death had been caused by a rupture of the aorta. In accordance with his wishes, Einstein's brain was preserved for medical research. He was cremated at Trenton, New Jersey, and his ashes scattered at a secret location.

In a macabre footnote to Einstein's death, a 1993 BBC documentary discovered that not only Einstein's brain had been removed for

The most beautiful experience we can have is the mysterious. It is the fundamental emotion which stands at the cradle of true art and true science. Whoever does not know it and can no longer wonder, no longer marvel, is as good as dead, and his eyes are dimmed. It was the experience of mystery – even if mixed with fear – that engendered religion. A knowledge of the existence of something we cannot penetrate, our perceptions of the profoundest reason and the most radiant beauty, which only in their most primitive forms are accessible to our minds – it is this knowledge and this emotion that constitute true religiosity; in this sense, and in this alone, I am a deeply religious man. I cannot conceive of a God who rewards and punishes his creatures, or has a will of the kind that we experience in ourselves. Neither can I nor would I want to conceive of an individual that survives his physical death; let feeble souls, from fear or absurd egoism, cherish such thoughts. I am satisfied with the mystery of the eternity of life and with the awareness and a glimpse of the marvellous structure of the existing world, together with the devoted striving to comprehend a portion, be it ever so tiny, of the Reason that manifests itself in nature.
ALBERT EINSTEIN, 'What I believe' (1930)[530]

IT IS TIME TO GO

Einstein in his study at Princeton

scientific study but also his eyes. Henry Abrams, Einstein's ophthalmologist, removed the eyes, which he now keeps in a safe deposit box. 'When you look into his eyes,' says Abrams, 'you're looking into the beauties and mysteries of the world.'[531]

Almost 50 years after his death, Einstein is still an instantly recognisable icon of science. Roland Barthes said that the 'myth of Einstein' can be traced to E=mc², the succinct formula that as if by magic unlocked the secrets of the universe.[532] With his wild hair and soulful eyes, Einstein became a modern magician in the popular imagination, a Faustian figure who dedicated his life to the search for the philosophers' stone, the formula of formulas: a final theory of everything. Like Marilyn Monroe or Che Guevara, Einstein has become an icon of the 20th century, his name synonymous with genius. It was the century of physics, a new physics that was strange beyond the wildest dreams of classical physicists like Newton. Relativity and quantum theory changed the way we think about the universe and Einstein was in the vanguard of these conceptual revolutions.

His complex character was, in Hans Albert's view, 'more like that of an artist than of a scientist'.[533] As Einstein himself said, science, the arts, and even religion share a common origin in the experience of the *mysterious*.[534] Music, in particular, expressed the sublime order of nature that Einstein sought to describe in mathematically beautiful theories: *Mozart's music is so pure and beautiful that I see it as a reflection of the inner beauty of the universe*.[535] His final project, the unified field theory, remained unfinished at his death, but recently scientists have resurrected his quest. Nowadays string theory represents the best candidate we have for a single, unified theory – a theory of everything. This revolutionary theory, rooted in quantum mechanics and the theories of relativity, is transforming our view of the universe today, just as Einstein's theories did at the beginning of the 20th century. String theory, with its multidimensional view of reality and particles that are really microscopic pieces of vibrating string, reaffirms the sublime complexity of the universe. As British physicist Stephen Hawking (b.1942) has said in response to Einstein's frequent criticism of quantum theory: 'God not only plays dice, but sometimes throws them where they cannot be seen.'[536]

A. Einstein.

Notes

The most authoritative source for Einstein's correspondence and writings is *The Collected Papers of Albert Einstein* (Princeton, 1987–). Volumes 1 to 8 out of an anticipated 25 volumes have been published to date, making available Einstein's writings up to 1921 and his correspondence up to 1918. In the following notes this is referred to as *CP* followed by volume and page number. Quotations from the translation supplements are indicated by 'trans' in the reference.

1 Quoted in A P French (ed), *Einstein: A Centenary Volume* (London, 1979), p. 199.
2 Hermann Hesse, 'Journey to Nuremberg' (1926), in: Hermann Hesse, *Autobiographical Writings*, ed Theodore Ziolkowski, trans Denver Lindley (London, 1973), p. 209.
3 'Ibid, p. 209.
4 Einstein to the editor of *Ulmer Abendpost*, 16 March 1929; in Albrecht Fölsing, *Albert Einstein: A Biography*, trans Ewald Osers (Harmondsworth, 1998), p. 8.
5 Einstein to Barbara Wilson, 7 January 1943; in Helen Dukas and Banesh Hoffmann (eds), *Albert Einstein, The Human Side: New Glimpses from his Archives* (Princeton, 1979), p. 8.
6 Maja Winteler-Einstein, 'Albert Einstein: A Biographical Sketch,' *CP* 1, *The Early Years, 1879–1902*, ed John Stachel et al (1987), trans Anna Beck, p. xvi.
7 Ibid, p. xvi.
8 Ibid, p. xv.
9 Ibid, p. xvi.
10 Ibid, p. xviii.
11 Ibid, p. xviii.
12 M K Wisehart, 'A Close Look at the World's Greatest Thinker', *American* (June 1930), p. 21; cited from Denis Brian, *Einstein: A Life* (New York, 1996), p. 194.
13 *CP* 1, trans, p. xvi.
14 Ibid, p. xvi.
15 Fritz Stern, *Dreams and Delusions: The Drama of German History* (London, 1987), p. 33.

16 Karl Raupp, 'Die Photographie in der modernen Kunst' (1889); in Reinhard Bauer and Ernst Piper (eds), *München* (Frankfurt am Main, 1986), p. 78.
17 Viktor Mann, *Wir waren fünf* (Konstanz, 1949); in Bauer and Piper (1986), p. 99.
18 Thomas Mann, *Collected Stories*, trans H T Lowe-Porter (London, 2001), pp. 153–6.
19 *CP* 1, trans, p. xvi.
20 Ibid, p. xvi–xvii.
21 Ibid, p. xvi.
22 Ibid, p. xvii.
23 Rudolph Kayser, who married Ilse Einstein, wrote under the pseudonym Anton Reiser: *Albert Einstein: A Biographical Portrait* (London, 1931), p. 29.
24 Carl Seelig, *Albert Einstein: A Documentary Biography*, trans Mervyn Savill (London, 1956), p. 11.
25 Einstein to Dr Hans Mühsam, 4 March 1953; in Fölsing (1998), p. 7.
26 Albert Einstein, *Autobiographical Notes: A Centennial Edition*, ed and trans Paul Arthur Schilpp (La Salle, 1979), p. 6; trans from Alice Calaprice (ed), *The Expanded Quotable Einstein* (Princeton, 2000), p. 15.
27 Ibid, p. 5.
28 Antonina Vallentin, *Einstein: A Biography*, trans Moura Budberg (London, 1954), p. 5.
29 Seelig (1956), p. 12.
30 Jette Koch to Pauline Einstein, 24 June 1881; in Banesh Hoffmann with Helen Dukas, *Albert Einstein* (St Albans, 1977), p. 13.
31 *CP* 1, trans, p. xviii.
32 Ibid, p. xviii; Einstein confirmed this

to Sybille Blinoff, 21 May 1954:
CP 1, p. lvii, n 37.

33 Ibid, p. xviii.

34 Einstein to James Franck, joint winner
of the 1926 Nobel Prize for Physics.
Seelig (1956), pp. 70–1.

35 *CP* 1, trans, p. xix.

36 Roger Highfield and Paul Carter, *The
Private Lives of Albert Einstein* (London,
1993), p. 11.

37 Highfield and Carter (1993), p. 9; 20
questions from Bela Kornitzer, 1948,
Clark archive, Edinburgh.

38 *CP* 1, p. lvi, n. 33.

39 Ibid, p. xviii.

40 Ibid, p. xviii.

41 Ibid, p. xviii.

42 Einstein to Philipp Frank, 1940;
Hoffmann (1975), p. 20; cf *CP* 1, p. lviii,
n. 39.

43 *CP* 1, trans, p. xix.

44 Seelig (1956), pp. 15–16.

45 Einstein, *Autobiographical Notes*, p. 9.

46 Ibid, p. 9.

47 Einstein, 'What I believe', *Forum and
Century* 84 (1930), pp. 193–4; from
French (1979), p. 304.

48 Einstein to Paul Plaut, 23 October 1928;
from Dukas and Hoffmann (1979),
p. 78.

49 Reiser (1931), p. 30.

50 Draft letter, 3 April 1920; *CP* 1, p. lx, n 44
(my trans).

51 Pauline Einstein to Fanny Einstein, 1
Aug 1886; *CP* 1, p. 3 (my trans).

52 Lewis Pyenson, *The Young Einstein: The
Advent of Relativity* (Bristol, 1985), p. 49.

53 *CP* 1, p. lviii, n 41.

54 Einstein, 'Autobiographische Skizze', in
Carl Seelig (ed), *Helle Zeit – Dunkle Zeit:
In Memoriam Albert Einstein* (Zurich,
1956), pp. 9–10.

55 Pyenson (1985), p. 3.

56 Einstein, *Autobiographical Notes*, p. 3.

57 *CP* 1, trans, p. xx.

58 Einstein, *Autobiographical Notes*, p. 3.

59 Einstein, *Autobiographical Notes*, p. 3.

60 Einstein to Beatrice Frohlich, 17
December 1952; Calaprice (2000),
p. 217.

61 Einstein, *Autobiographical Notes*, p. 5.

62 Einstein to an admirer, 24 March 1954;
Dukas and Hoffmann (1979), p. 43.

63 Ibid, p. 15.

64 Jürgen Renn and Robert Schulmann
(eds), *Albert Einstein/Mileva Marić: The
Love Letters*, trans Shawn Smith
(Princeton, 1992), p. xxiii.

65 Brian (1996), p. 4; cf Alexander

Moszkowski, *Conversations with Einstein*,
trans Henry L Brose (London, 1972),
pp. 223–4.

66 Einstein, *Autobiographical Notes*, p. 9; my
trans.

67 Maja Winteler-Einstein, *CP* 1, trans,
p. xx.

68 Einstein, *Autobiographical Notes*, p. 9.

69 Bertrand Russell, *The Autobiography of
Bertrand Russell*, vol 1 (London, 1967),
p. 36.

70 Einstein, 'On the method of theoretical
physics', in French (1979), p. 311.

71 *CP* 1, trans, p. xx.

72 Maja Winteler-Einstein; *CP* 1, trans,
p. xxi.

73 Einstein to Philipp Frank, 1940; *CP* 1,
p. lxiii, n 56 (my trans).

74 Einstein in 1933; Hoffmann (1975), p. 26.

75 Maja Winteler-Einstein; *CP* 1, trans,
p. xxi.

76 *CP* 1, trans, p. xvii.

77 Ibid, p. 123.

78 Hans Albert Einstein in Bela Kornitzer,
Ladies Home Journal (April 1951), p. 136;
Brian (1996), p. 7.

79 *CP* 1, trans, p. xxii.

80 See Leonhard Sohncke, 'Die
Umwälzung unserer Anschauungen
vom Wesen der elektrischen
Wirkungen', in *Himmel und Erde:
Illustrirte naturwissenschaftliche
Monatsschrift* 3 (1891): pp. 157–172.

81 Albin Herzog to Gustav Maier, 25
September 1895; *CP* 1, trans, p. 7.

82 Seelig (1956), p. 21.

83 *CP* 1, trans, p. xxii.

84 Ibid, p. 22.

85 Ibid, p. 10.

86 Seelig (1956), p. 14.

87 Ibid, p. 15.

88 J Ryffel, 31 March 1896; *CP* 1, trans, p. 12.

89 Seelig (1956), pp. 13–4, 42; cf p. 40.

90 Ibid, p. 19.

91 Ibid, pp. 18–19.

92 21 April 1896; *CP* 1, trans, p. 12.

93 *CP* 1, trans, pp. 12–13.

94 Ibid, pp. 12–13.

95 Vallentin (1954), p. 3.

96 18 September 1896; *CP* 1, trans,
pp. 15–16.

97 Marie Winteler to Einstein, 4–25
November 1896; *CP* 1, trans, p. 29.

98 *CP* 1, trans, p. 30.

99 30 November 1896; *CP* 1, trans, p. 31.

100 21 April 1896; *CP* 1, trans, p. 13.

101 13 December 1896; *CP* 1, trans, p. 31.

102 Einstein to Pauline Winteler, May 1897;
CP 1, trans, p. 32.

103 Ibid, pp. 32–3.
104 Einstein to Pauline Winteler, 7 June 1897; CP 1, trans, p. 33.
105 May 1897; CP 1, trans, p. 33.
106 Einstein to Mileva Marić, 28 September 1899; Renn and Schulmann (1992), p. 16.
107 CP 1, p. 385 (my trans).
108 Seelig (1956), p. 41.
109 Ibid, p. 14.
110 Ibid, p. 37.
111 Ibid, p. 38.
112 Einstein to Mileva, 4 April 1901; CP 1, trans, p. 162.
113 Seelig (1956), p. 34.
114 Einstein to Anna Grossmann, 26 September 1936; Fölsing (1998), p. 53.
115 Einstein, 'Autobiographische Skizze', p. 10.
116 Ibid, p. 10 (my trans).
117 Seelig (1956), p. 30.
118 Einstein to Julia Niggli, 28 July 1899; CP 1, trans, p. 128.
119 Seelig (1956), pp. 40–1.
120 Vallentin (1954), p. 19.
121 Seelig (1956), p. 28.
122 Cited by Maurice Solovine, Albert Einstein: Lettres à Maurice Solovine (Paris, 1956), p. vii; in French (1979), p. 9.
123 Einstein, Autobiographical Notes, p. 15.
124 Ibid, p. 17.
125 Ibid, p. 31.
126 Ibid, p. 31.
127 Ibid, p. 25.
128 Seelig (1956), p. 29.
129 Einstein, Autobiographical Notes, p. 19.
130 Ibid, p. 19.
131 Seelig (1956), p. 30.
132 Ibid, p. 30.
133 CP 1, trans, p. xix.
134 Pyenson (1985), p. 58.
135 Renn and Schulmann (1992), p. xxi.
136 Einstein to Heinrich Zangger, June 1912; CP 5, The Swiss Years: Correspondence, 1902–1914, ed Martin J Klein et al (1993), p. 480 (my trans).
137 Einstein, 'What I believe'; from Calaprice (2000), p. 11.
138 Highfield and Carter (1993), p. 3.
139 Einstein to Paul Ehrenfest, 12 April 1926; Dukas and Hoffmann (1979), p. 63.
140 Einstein to Mileva, August 1899; CP 1, trans, p. 129.
141 Mileva to Einstein, 20 October 1897; Renn and Schulmann (1992), p. 3.
142 Einstein to Mileva, 16 February 1898; ibid, p. 5.
143 Einstein to Mileva, 13 or 20 March 1899; CP 1, trans, p. 126.
144 Einstein to Mileva, 10 September 1899; ibid, p. 133.
145 Einstein to Mileva, August 1899; Renn and Schulmann (1992), p. 9.
146 Einstein to Mileva, 10 August 1899; ibid, p. 11.
147 Dennis Overbye, Einstein in Love: A Scientific Romance (London, 2001), p. 20.
148 Einstein to Mileva, 3 October 1900; Renn and Schulmann (1992), p. 36.
149 Desanka Trbuhović-Gjurić, Im Schatten Albert Einsteins: Das tragische Leben der Mileva Einstein-Marić (Bern, 1983), p. 53; from Overbye (2001), p. 32.
150 Ibid, p. 32.
151 Seelig (1956), p. 38.
152 Ibid, p. 38.
153 Einstein to Mileva, 13 or 20 March 1899; Renn and Schulmann (1992), p. 8.
154 Milana Bota, 3 June 1898; from Michele Zackheim, Einstein's Daughter: The Search for Lieserl (New York, 1999), p. 18.
155 Letters dated respectively 28 November 1898, August 1899, 10 October 1899 and early 1900; CP 1, trans, pp. 125, 129, 136, 138.
156 Einstein to Mileva, 10 August 1899; Renn and Schulmann (1992), p. 10.
157 Peter Michelmore, Einstein: Profile of the Man (London, 1963), p. 32.
158 Einstein to Mileva, 13 or 20 March 1899; Renn and Schulmann (1992), p. 7.
159 Einstein to Mileva, 28 September 1899; ibid, p. 16.
160 Einstein to Mileva, 10 August 1899; ibid, pp. 10–11.
161 Mileva to Helene Kaufler, 9 March 1900; CP 1, trans, p. 139.
162 Einstein to Mileva, 29 July 1900; Renn and Schulmann (1992), p. 19.
163 Einstein to Mileva, 29 July 1900; ibid, p. 19.
164 Einstein to Mileva, 29 July 1900; ibid, pp. 19–20.
165 Einstein to Mileva, early September 1900; ibid, p. 29.
166 Einstein to Mileva, 14 August and 3 October 1900; ibid, pp. 26, 35.
167 Einstein to Mileva, 9 August 1900; ibid, p. 24.
168 Einstein to Mileva, 14 August 1900; ibid, p. 26.
169 Einstein to Mileva, 13 September 1900; ibid, p. 31.
170 Einstein to Mileva, 13 September 1900; ibid, p. 32.
171 Einstein to Mileva, 9 August and 13 September 1900; ibid, pp. 25, 32.
172 Einstein to Helene Kaufler, 11 October 1900; CP 1, trans, p. 153.

173 Ibid, p. 27.

174 Mileva to Helene Savić (neé Kaufler), 11 December 1900; *CP* 1, trans, p. 154.

175 Mileva to Helene Savić (neé Kaufler), 20 December 1900; ibid, p. 156.

176 Mileva to Helene Savić, 20 December 1900; ibid, p. 156.

177 Einstein to Johannes Stark, 7 December 1907; *CP* 5, p. 79.

178 Einstein to Mileva, 4 April 1901; Renn and Schulmann (1992), p. 42.

179 Mileva to Helene Savić, spring 1901; *CP* 1, trans, p. 157.

180 Mileva to Helene Savić, November/December 1901; ibid, p. 183.

181 Einstein to Mileva, 15 April 1901; ibid, p. 166.

182 Einstein to Mileva, 30 April 1901; Renn and Schulmann (1992), p. 46.

183 Ibid, p. 47.

184 Mileva to Helene Savić, May 1901; *CP* 1, trans, p. 172.

185 Mileva to Helene Savić, May 1901; ibid, p. 172.

186 Mileva to Einstein, May 1901; Renn and Schulmann (1992), p. 52.

187 Einstein to Mileva, 28 May 1901; ibid, p. 54.

188 Einstein to Mileva, 4 June 1901; ibid, p. 55.

189 Mileva to Einstein, 8 July 1901; ibid, p. 58.

190 Mileva to Einstein, 31 July 1901; ibid, p. 60.

191 Milana Bota, 4 November 1901; Zackheim (1999), p. 31.

192 Mileva to Einstein, 13 November 1901; Renn and Schulmann (1992), p. 63.

193 Mileva to Helene Savić, November/December 1901; *CP* 1, trans, p. 183.

194 Mileva to Helene Savić, November/December 1901; ibid, p. 183.

195 Einstein to Mileva, 17 December 1901; Renn and Schulmann (1992), p. 69.

196 Einstein to Mileva, 28 November 1901; ibid, p. 65.

197 Einstein to Mileva, 17 December 1901; ibid, p. 70.

198 Einstein to Mileva, 12 December 1901; ibid, p. 68.

199 Einstein to Mileva, 12 December 1901; ibid, p. 68.

200 Mileva to Einstein, 13 November 1901; ibid, p. 64.

201 Einstein to Mileva, 19 December 1901; ibid, p. 71.

202 Einstein to Mileva, 28 December 1901; ibid, p. 72.

203 Einstein to Mileva, 28 December 1901; ibid, p. 73.

204 Einstein to Mileva, 4 February 1902; ibid, p. 73.

205 Einstein to Mileva, 4 February 1902; ibid, pp. 73–4.

206 Einstein to Mileva, 19 September 1903; ibid, p. 78.

207 Zackheim (1999), p. 259.

208 Einstein to Mileva, 4 February 1902; Renn and Schulmann (1992), p. 74.

209 Einstein to Mileva, 4 February 1902; ibid, p. 74.

210 Talmud referred to this in his popular account of Einstein's science, which he wrote under the name of Max Talmey: *The Relativity Theory Simplified and the Formative Period of Its Inventor* (New York, 1932), pp. 166–7.

211 Einstein to Pauline Winteler, 21 May 1897; *CP* 5, trans, p. 3.

212 Pauline Einstein to Pauline Winteler, 20 February 1902; *CP* 1, trans, p. 193.

213 Einstein to Hans Wohlwend, 15 August – 3 October 1902; *CP* 5, trans, p. 5.

214 Solovine (1956); in French (1979), p. 9.

215 Ibid, p. 9.

216 Ibid, p. 9.

217 Seelig (1956), p. 57.

218 W I B Beveridge, *The Art of Scientific Investigation* (New York, 1950), p. 77; from Brian (1996), p. 46.

219 Einstein, *Autobiographical Notes*, p. 13.

220 Ernst Mach, *The Science of Mechanics* (1883); from Gerald Holton, 'Mach, Einstein and the search for reality', in Colin Chant and John Fauvel (eds), *Darwin to Einstein: Historical Studies on Science and Belief* (Burnt Mill, 1980), p. 237.

221 Henri Poincaré, *Science and Hypothesis* (New York, 1952), p. 90; from Overbye (2001), p. 104.

222 Solovine (1956), p. x; from Arthur I Miller, *Einstein, Picasso: Space, Time, and the Beauty That Causes Havoc* (New York, 2001), p. 76.

223 Cited from Silvio Bergia, 'Einstein and the Birth of Special Relativity,' in French (1979), p. 80.

224 Brian (1996), p. 51.

225 Einstein to Mileva, 28 June 1902; Renn and Schulmann (1992), p. 77.

226 Michelmore (1963), p. 38.

227 Einstein to Hans Wohlwend, 15 August to 3 October 1902; *CP* 5, trans, p. 4.

228 Einstein to Carl Seelig, 5 May 1952; Fölsing (1998), p. 106.

229 Einstein to Michele Besso, 22 January 1903; *CP* 5, trans, p. 7.
230 Einstein to Hans Wohlwend, 15 August to 3 October 1902; ibid, p. 5.
231 Mileva to Helene Savić, 20 March 1903; ibid, n 7.
232 Seelig (1956), p. 46.
233 Mileva to Einstein, 27 August 1903; Renn and Schulmann (1992), p. 78.
234 Einstein to Mileva, 19 September 1903; ibid, p. 78.
235 Abraham Pais, *'Subtle is the Lord . . .': The Science and the Life of Albert Einstein* (Oxford, 1982), p. 68.
236 Einstein to Conrad Habicht, 15 April 1904; *CP* 5, trans, p. 17.
237 Einstein, *Autobiographical Notes*, p. 49 (trans modified).
238 Einstein to Conrad Habicht, 6 March 1905; *CP* 5, trans, p. 19.
239 Einstein to Conrad Habicht, 30 June – 22 September 1905; ibid, p. 20.
240 Seelig (1956), p. 56 (trans modified).
241 Einstein to Mileva, 4 April 1901; Renn and Schulmann (1992), p. 41.
242 Seelig (1956), p. 71.
243 Ibid, p. 71.
244 Michelmore (1963), p. 39.
245 Einstein to Conrad Habicht, 18 or 25 May 1905; *CP* 5, trans, p. 20.
246 Hoffmann (1975), p. 49.
247 Ibid, p. 47.
248 Einstein, 'Über einen die Erzeugung und Verwandlung des Lichtes betreffenden heuristischen Gesichtspunkt' ('On a Heuristic Point of View Concerning the Production and Transformation of Light') in John Stachel et al (eds and trans), *Einstein's Miraculous Year: Five Papers That Changed the Face of Physics* (Princeton, 1998), p. 173.
249 Nernst to A Schuster, 17 March 1910; Fölsing (1998), p. 154.
250 Einstein, *Autobiographical Notes*, p. 45.
251 Einstein to Besso, 22 January 1903; *CP* 5, trans, p. 7.
252 Stachel (1998), pp. 36–7.
253 Hoffmann (1975), p. 57.
254 Einstein, 'Über die von der molekularkinetischen Theorie der Wärme geforderte Bewegung von in ruhenden Flüssigkeiten suspendierten Teilchen' ('On the Motion of Small Particles Suspended in Liquids at Rest Required by the Molecular-Kinetic Theory of Heat'), Stachel (1998), p. 85.
255 Einstein, 'On the Motion of Small Particles', Stachel (1998), p. 85.
256 Thanks to Graham Nelson for this latter point.
257 Einstein, 'Zur Elektrodynamik bewegter Körper' ('On the Electrodynamics of Moving Bodies'), Stachel (1998), p. 123.
258 Alan Lightman, *Great Ideas in Physics* (New York, 1992), p. 114.
259 Hoffmann (1975), p. 69.
260 Einstein, 'On the Electrodynamics of Moving Bodies', Stachel (1998), p. 123.
261 Einstein, 'Grundgedanken und Methoden der Relitivitätstheorie, in ihrer Entwicklung dargestellt' ('Fundamental Ideas and Methods of the Theory of Relativity, Presented in Their Development'), (January 1920, draft of unpublished article) *CP* 7, *The Berlin Years: Writings, 1918–1921*, ed Michel Janssen et al (2002), p. 264.
262 Einstein, 'Fundamental Ideas and Methods of the Theory of Relativity', *CP* 7, pp. 264–5 (my trans).
263 Paul Schilpp (ed), *Albert Einstein: Philosopher-Scientist* (Evanston, Ill, 1949), pp. 19–20; from Fölsing (1998), p. 173.
264 Einstein, *Autobiographical Notes*, p. 49.
265 Einstein, 'On the Electrodynamics of Moving Bodies'; Stachel (1998), p. 124.
266 Miller (2001), p. 199.
267 Einstein, *Autobiographical Notes*, pp. 49–51.
268 Einstein, *Autobiographical Notes*, p. 31.
269 Einstein, 'On the Electrodynamics of Moving Bodies'; Stachel (1998), p. 124.
270 J C Maxwell, 'A Dynamical Theory of the Electromagnetic Field' (1864).
271 Einstein 'On the Electrodynamics of Moving Bodies', p. 124.
272 Einstein, *Autobiographical Notes*, p. 23.
273 Isaac Newton, *Principia Mathematica* (1687), trans A Motte (Berkeley, 1962), p. 6; from Lightman (1992), p. 153.
274 Einstein, *Autobiographical Notes*, p. 31.
275 *The Ascent of Man* (London: Book Club Associates, 1979), pp. 247–8, 249–52.
276 *Relativity: The Special and the General Theory. A Popular Exposition* (1916), trans Robert W Lawson (London, 1960), p. 55.
277 Einstein to Conrad Habicht, 30 June to 22 September 1905; *CP* 5, trans, p. 20.
278 Einstein to Conrad Habicht, 30 June to 22 September 1905; ibid, p. 21.
279 Einstein, 'Ist die Trägheit eines Körpers von seinem Energieinhalt abhängig?' ('Does the Inertia of a Body Depend on its Energy Content?'); Stachel (1998), p. 164.

280 Ibid, p. 164.
281 Einstein, 'E=mc²' (1946); in Albert Einstein, *Out of My Later Years* (New York, 1950), p. 53.
282 Michelmore (1963), pp. 41–2.
283 Ibid, p. 42.
284 Einstein to Mileva, 27 March 1901; cf 15 April 1901; Renn and Schulmann (1992), pp. 39 and 45.
285 Einstein, 'On the Electrodynamics of Moving Bodies'; Stachel (1998), p. 159.
286 Friedrich Haller, official memorandum, January 1906; CP 5, p. 39, n 1.
287 Einstein to Solovine, 27 April 1906; CP 5, trans, p. 25.
288 Pais (1982), p. 47.
289 Seelig (1956), p. 78.
290 Ibid, p. 78.
291 Max Laue to Jakob Laub, 2 September 1907; CP 5, p. 74, n 11.
292 Einstein to Alfred Schnauder, spring 1907; ibid, p. 28.
293 Jakob Laub to Einstein, 1 March 1908; ibid, p. 63.
294 Seelig (1956), p. 88.
295 Friedrich Adler to Victor Adler, 1 July 1908; Fölsing (1998), p. 248.
296 Einstein to Laub, 19 May 1909; CP 5, trans, p. 120.
297 Hermann Minkowski, 'Raum und Zeit', *Physikalische Zeitschrift* 20 (1908), p. 104.
298 Einstein to Laub, 19 May 1909; CP 5, trans, p. 120.
299 Einstein, 'Über die Entwickelung unserer Anschauungen über das Wesen und die Konstitution der Strahlung' ('On the Development of our Views Concerning the Nature and Constitution of Radiation') (presented 21 September 1909); CP 2, *The Swiss Years: Writings, 1900–1909*, ed John Stachel (1989), trans Anna Beck, p. 379.
300 Ibid, p. 379.
301 Wolfgang Pauli, 'Einstein's Contribution to Quantum Theory', in Schilpp (1949); Fölsing (1998), p. 257.
302 Einstein to Maja Einstein, after February 1899; CP 1, trans, p. 126.
303 Friedrich Adler to Victor Adler, October 1910; Ronald W Clark, *Einstein: The Life and Times* (New York, 1971), p. 132.
304 Mileva to Helene Savić, 3 September 1909; from John Stachel, 'Albert Einstein and Mileva Marić: A Collaboration that Failed to Develop', *Creative Couples in the Sciences*, eds Helena M Pycior et al (New Brunswick, 1996), p. 211.

305 Einstein to Anna Schmid, August 1899; CP 1, trans, p. 128.
306 Einstein to Anna Meyer-Schmid, 12 May 1909; CP 5, trans, p. 115.
307 Mileva to Georg Meyer, 23 May 1909; ibid, p. 199, n 4.
308 Einstein to Georg Meyer, 7 June 1909; ibid, trans, p. 127.
309 Einstein to Besso, 17 November 1909; ibid, trans, p. 140.
310 Einstein to Erika Schaerer-Meyer, 27 July 1951; ibid, p. 199, n 4.
311 Mileva to Helene Savić, October 1909; Stachel (1996), p. 211.
312 Einstein to Julia Niggli, 6 August 1899; CP 1, trans, pp. 129–30.
313 Einstein, 'Das Gemeinsame am künstlerischen und wissenschaftlichen Erleben' ('The Common Element in Artistic and Scientific Achievement') in *Menschen. Zeitschrift neuer Kunst* 4 (1921), p. 19; CP 7, p. 380 (my trans).
314 Einstein, 'Motive des Forschens' ('Motives for Research'), lecture delivered on Max Planck's 60th birthday, 26 April 1918; CP 7, p. 55 (my trans).
315 Einstein, 'Motives for Research'; CP 7, p. 56 (my trans).
316 David Reichinstein, in Michelmore (1963), p. 47.
317 Quoted by Paul Ehrenfest, letter to Tatiana Ehrenfest, 25 February 1912; CP 5, p. 254, n 3.
318 Student petition to retain Einstein at the University of Zurich, 23 June 1910; ibid, trans, p. 156.
319 Hans Tanner in Seelig (1956), p. 100.
320 Seelig (1956), p. 102.
321 Einstein to Laub, 11 October 1910; CP 5, trans, p. 164.
322 Einstein to Heinrich Zangger, 27 January 1912; ibid, trans, p. 250.
323 Einstein to Hendrik A Lorentz, 27 January 1911; ibid, trans, p. 175.
324 Einstein cited in G L de Haas-Lorentz (ed), *H A Lorentz: Impressions of His Life and Work* (Amsterdam, 1957), p. 8.
325 Ibid, pp. 102–3.
326 Einstein to Friedrich Adler, 9 February 1911; CP 5, p. 279 (my trans).
327 Einstein to Marcel Grossmann, 27 April 1911; ibid, trans, pp. 186–7.
328 Michelmore (1963), p. 49.
329 Einstein to Hans Tanner, 24 April 1911; CP 5, trans, p. 186.
330 Einstein to Alfred and Clara Stern, 17 March 1912; ibid, trans, p. 275.
331 Einstein to Besso, 13 May 1911; ibid, trans, p. 187.

332 Philipp Frank, *Einstein: His Life and Times*, ed Shuichi Kusaka, trans George Rosen (New York, 1947), p. 98.

333 Poincaré to the Federal Technical University, November 1911; Seelig (1956), p. 135.

334 Einstein to Alfred and Clara Stern, 2 February 1912; *CP 5*, trans, p. 255.

335 Einstein to A and C Stern, 17 March 1912; ibid, trans, p. 275.

336 Einstein to Besso, 26 March 1912; ibid, trans, p. 276.

337 Einstein to Besso, 26 March 1912; ibid, trans, p. 279.

338 Einstein to Carl Seelig, 5 May 1952; Overbye (2001), p. 201.

339 Einstein to Elsa Löwenthal, 7 May 1912; *CP 5*, trans, p. 293.

340 Einstein to Carl Seelig, 5 May 1952; Fölsing (1998), p. 297.

341 Einstein to Elsa Löwenthal, 30 April 1912; *CP 5*, trans, p. 292.

342 Einstein to Elsa Löwenthal, 30 April 1912; ibid, trans, p. 292.

343 Einstein to Elsa Löwenthal, 30 April 1912; ibid, trans, p. 292.

344 Einstein to Arnold Sommerfeld, 29 October 1912; ibid, trans, p. 324.

345 Einstein to Ehrenfest, 28 May 1913; ibid, trans, p. 334.

346 Einstein to Elsa Löwenthal, 14 July 1913; ibid, trans, p. 341.

347 Einstein to Elsa Löwenthal, end July 1913; ibid, trans, p. 343.

348 Einstein to Louis Kollros; Michelmore (1963), p. 55.

349 Einstein to Elsa Löwenthal, 14 July 1913; ibid, trans, p. 341.

350 Einstein to Heinrich Zangger, 7 July 1915; *CP 8, The Berlin Years: Correspondence, 1914–1918*, ed Robert Schulmann et al (1998), trans Ann M Hentschel, p. 110.

351 Einstein to Elsa, November / December 1913; *CP 5*, trans, p. 365.

352 Einstein to Elsa, early February 1914; ibid, trans, p. 379.

353 Einstein to Elsa, early February 1914; ibid, trans, p. 379.

354 Memorandum, Einstein to Mileva, 18 July 1914; *CP 8*, trans, pp. 32–3.

355 Einstein to Heinrich Zangger, 10 April 1915; ibid, trans, p. 88.

356 Einstein to Elsa, 3 August 1914; ibid, trans, p. 40.

357 Einstein to Mileva, 15 September 1914; ibid, trans, p. 42.

358 Einstein, 'Meine Meinung über den Krieg' ('My Opinion of the War'), (October 1915) in *Das Land Goethes 1914–1916: Ein vaterländisches Gedenkbuch* (Berlin, 1916); *CP 6, The Berlin Years: Writings, 1914–1917*, eds A J Kox et al (1996), trans Alfred Engel, p. 96.

359 Einstein to Zangger, 10 April 1915; *CP 8*, trans, p. 87.

360 Einstein, 'Über den Einfluß der Schwerkraft auf die Ausbreitung des Lichtes' ('On the Influence of Gravitation on the Propagation of Light') (1911); *CP 3, The Swiss Years: Writings, 1909–1911*, eds Martin J Klein et al (1993), trans Anna Beck, p. 379.

361 Einstein to Ehrenfest, early March 1914; *CP 5*, trans, p. 380.

362 Hoffmann (1975), p. 124.

363 Einstein to Ehrenfest, 17 January 1916; *CP 8*, trans, p. 179.

364 Max Born in Brian (1996), p. 91.

365 Einstein's Kyoto lecture, 14 December 1922; trans from notes taken by Yon Ishiwara by Y A Ono, *Physics Today*, August 1932; Calaprice (2000), pp. 242–3.

366 Einstein, 'Fundamental Ideas and Methods of the Theory of Relativity, Presented in Their Development', (January 1920) *CP 7*, p. 265 (my trans).

367 Hoffmann (1975), p. 120.

368 Brian (1996), p. 91.

369 Hoffmann (1975), p. 122.

370 Einstein, 'Kosmologische Betrachtungen zur Allgemeinen Relativitätstheorie' ('Cosmological Considerations in the General Theory of Relativity'), *CP 6*, trans, pp. 430–1.

371 George Gamow, *My World Line: An Informal Autobiography* (New York, 1970), p. 150.

372 Jocelyn Bell Burnell, interview in Melvyn Bragg with Ruth Gardiner, *On Giants' Shoulders: Great Scientists and Their Discoveries from Archimedes to DNA* (London, 1998), p. 289.

373 Seelig (1956), p. 84.

374 Diary of Rudolf Jakob Humm, May 1917; Seelig (1956), p. 156 (trans modified).

375 Einstein, 'Zur Quantentheorie der Strahlung' ('On the Quantum Theory of Radiation'); *CP 6*, trans, p. 232 (trans modified).

376 Einstein to Besso, 9 March 1917; *CP 8*, trans, p. 293 (trans modified).

377 Einstein to Besso, 21 July 1916; ibid, trans, p. 234.

378 Einstein to Zangger, 26 July 1916; ibid, trans, p. 238.

379 Evelyn Einstein in Overbye (2001), p. 278.

380 Einstein to Helene Savić, 8 September 1916; *CP* 8, trans, p. 250.

381 Einstein to Besso, 22 September 1917; ibid, trans, p. 374.

382 Ilse Einstein to Georg Nicolai, 22 May 1918, marked 'Please destroy this letter immediately after reading it'; ibid, trans, p. 564.

383 Conversation with Esther Salaman, spring 1924; Fölsing (1998), p. 428.

384 Evelyn Einstein in Overbye (2001), p. 228.

385 Vallentin (1954), p. 121.

386 Ibid, p. 47.

387 Samuel Johnson Woolf, 'Einstein at 50', *New York Times*, 18 August 1929; from Brian (1996), p. 182.

388 Frank (1947), p. 124 (trans modified).

389 Einstein, 'On the Influence of Gravitation on the Propagation of Light' (1911); *CP* 3, trans, p. 379.

390 *Relativity: The Special and the General Theory. A Popular Exposition*, trans Robert W Lawson (London, 1920), p. 75.

391 Hoffmann (1975), p. 129.

392 *Observatory* 42 (1919): pp. 389–98; from Fölsing (1998), p. 444.

393 *The Times*, 7 November 1919, p. 12.

394 Alfred North Whitehead, *Science and the Modern World* (Cambridge, 1927), pp. 12–13 (based on the Lowell Lectures, 1925).

395 A S Eddington to Einstein, 1 December 1919; Hoffmann (1975), p. 133.

396 *New York Times*, 16 November 1919.

397 *The Times*, 18 November 1919, editorial.

398 Einstein, 'Einstein on His Theory: Time, Space, and Gravitation', *The Times*, 28 November 1919, pp. 13–14; *CP* 7, pp. 212–5.

399 Moszkowski (1972), pp. 13–14.

400 Seelig (1956), p. 80.

401 Michelmore (1962), p. 82.

402 Einstein to Zangger, early March 1920; Calaprice (2000), p. 48.

403 Einstein to Max Born, early March 1920; Hoffmann (1975), p. 135.

404 Stern (1987), p. 46.

405 Paul Weyland's 'Working Association of German Natural Scientists for the Preservation of Pure Science' held its first public rally in Berlin on 24 August 1920; *CP* 7, p. 105.

406 Einstein to Ehrenfest, before 10 September 1920; ibid, p. 107.

407 'One ought to seize this Jew by the gullet,' was one comment reported

by *Die Umschau* 24 (1920), p. 554; ibid, p. 348, n 3.

408 Einstein, 'Meine Antwort. Über die anti-relativitätstheoretische Gmbh' ('My Response. On the Anti-Relativity Company') *Berliner Tageblatt*, 27 August 1920; ibid, pp. 344–9.

409 Six lectures were given at the conference of the Gesellschaft Deutscher Naturforscher und Ärzte, 23–4 September 1920 at Bad Nauheim, followed by a debate held at Einstein's request. Various accounts of the argument between Einstein and Lenard exist; this remark appears in *Berliner Tageblatt*, 24 September 1920; ibid, p. 358, n 16.

410 Einstein to Max von Laue, 26 May 1933; Stern (1987), p. 27.

411 Stern (1987), p. 40.

412 Einstein to Willy Hellpach, October 1929; Fölsing (1998), p. 488.

413 Einstein, *The World as I See It*, trans Alan Harris (New York, 1934), p. 90.

414 *CP* 7, p. xxxix.

415 Einstein, *About Zionism*, trans Leon Simon (London, 1930); from French (1979), p. 201.

416 Einstein to Heinrich York-Steiner, 19 November 1929; *CP* 7, p. 228.

417 Einstein, 'Zur Errichtung der hebräischen Universität in Jerusalem' ('On the Founding of the Hebrew University in Jerusalem'), *Jüdische Pressezentrale Zürich*, 26 August 1921, p. 1; ibid, p. 446 (my trans).

418 K Blumenfeld to Chaim Weizmann, 16 March 1921; Fölsing (1998), p. 498.

419 Ibid, p. 498.

420 Werner Heisenberg, *Physics and Beyond: Encounters and Conversations*, trans Arnold J Pomerans (London, 1971), p. 84.

421 Seelig (1956), p. 154.

422 Seelig (1956), p. 81.

423 Hoffmann (1975), p. 95.

424 'Einstein Tells Why He Can't Explain', *Boston Globe*, 18 May 1921, pp. 1, 6; Brian (1996), p. 130.

425 Vallentin (1954), p. 69.

426 Brian (1996), p. 123.

427 *Collected Poems* (New Directions, 1938).

429 Einstein to Besso, end of May 1921; French (1979), p. 203.

429 Einstein's travel diary, 3 February 1923; Calaprice (2000), p. 129.

430 Apollinaire, *Méditations esthétiques*, trans Lionel Abel (1948). Cited in George Heard Hamilton, *Painting and Sculpture*

in Europe 1880–1940 (Penguin, 1983) p. 534 n 241.5.

431 István Hargittai, The Road to Stockholm: Nobel Prizes, Science, and Scientists (Oxford, 2002), p. 305.

432 Ibid, p. 305.

433 Einstein, Autobiographical Notes, p. 43.

434 French (1979), p. 22.

435 Einstein, Autobiographical Notes, p. 49.

436 Manjit Kumar, 'Quantum Reality', Prometheus 2 (1999), pp. 58.

437 Alan J Friedman and Carol C Donley, Einstein as Myth and Muse (Cambridge, 1985), p. 119.

438 Einstein to Born, 4 December 1926; Max Born (ed), The Born–Einstein Letters, trans Irene Born (New York, 1971), p. 91.

439 Cited in Kumar (1999), pp. 58.

440 Einstein, Autobiographical Notes, p. 49.

441 Heisenberg (1971), pp. 80–1.

442 French (1979), p. 133.

443 Ibid, pp. 133, 150.

444 Einstein to Besso, 5 January 1929; Fölsing (1998), p. 601.

445 Einstein to Maja Winteler-Einstein, 22 October 1929; Einstein, 'Théorie unitaire du champ physique' ('Unified Physical Field Theory'); ibid, p. 606.

446 Pais (1982), p. 320.

447 Charles Nordmann, in L'Illustration, 15 April 1922; Fölsing (1998), p. 548.

448 Einstein to Besso, 28 May 1921; ibid, p. 428.

449 Elsa Einstein to Hermann Struck, 1929; ibid, p. 429.

450 Frank (1947), p. 221.

451 Elsa to Maja, 19 August 1929; Fölsing (1998), p. 612.

452 Vallentin (1954), p. 120.

453 Ibid, p. 120.

454 Brian (1996), p. 180.

455 Vallentin (1954), p. 141.

456 Ibid, pp. 141–2.

457 Dukas and Hoffman (1979), p. 63.

458 Einstein to Jewish Telegraph Agency, 18 September 1930; Fölsing (1998), p. 629.

459 Heisenberg (1971), p. 62.

460 Vallentin (1954), p. 151.

461 Frank (1947), p. 226.

462 A Flexner to Einstein, 13 October 1933; Abraham Pais, Einstein Lived Here (Oxford, 1994), p. 196.

463 Einstein to Prussian Academy of Sciences, 28 March 1933; Fölsing (1998), p. 661.

464 Berliner Lokalanzeiger, 17 March 1933; Fölsing (1998), p. 661.

465 See P Lenard, Deutsche Physik in vier Bänden (Munich, 1936–7), I, Einleitung und Mechanik, p. ix.

466 Max Planck to Heinrich von Ficker, 31 March 1933; Christa Kirstin and H-J Treder, Albert Einstein in Berlin, 1913–1933 (Berlin, 1979).

467 Clark (1971), p. 494.

468 3 October 1933; Pais (1994), p. 195.

469 Joseph Rotblat, 'Einstein the Pacifist Warrior', in Maurice Goldsmith, et al (eds), Einstein: The First Hundred Years (Oxford, 1980), p. 104.

470 Einstein to a Belgian pacifist, New York Times, 10 September 1933; Pais (1994), p. 194.

471 Rotblat (1980), p. 105.

472 Einstein to a pacifist, September 1933; Otto Nathan and Heinz Norden (eds), Einstein on Peace (New York, 1960), p. 235.

473 Brian (1996), p. 297.

474 'Women Patriots Try New Ban on Einstein', New York Times, 9 January 1933; Brian (1996), p. 241.

475 Einstein, Ideas and Opinions, trans Sonja Bargmann (New York, 1954), p. 7.

476 Ed Regis, Who Got Einstein's Office? Eccentricity and Genius at the Institute for Advanced Study (Reading, Mass, 1987), p. 4.

477 Robert Jungk, Brighter than a Thousand Suns (New York, 1958), p. 46; Brian (1996), p. 237.

478 Dutch-language interview with Einstein, 29 June 1921 (publ in Nieuwe Rotterdamsche Courant, 4 July 1921); CP 7, p. 625.

479 Seelig (1956), p. 204.

480 Vallentin (1954), pp. 170–1.

481 Seelig (1956), p. 204.

482 Einstein to Oscar Veblen, May 1921, on hearing reports of an experiment that supposedly disproved his theory of gravitation; it can now be seen at 202 Jones Hall; Calaprice (2000), p. 241.

483 Interview with Banesh Hoffmann, 6 September 1985; Brian (1996), p. 297.

484 Einstein to Elsbeth Grossmann, 26 September 1936; Seelig (1956), p. 208.

485 Einstein to Maja, 1936; Brian (1996), p. 289.

486 Einstein to Born, early 1937; Born (1971), p. 128.

487 Seelig (1956), p. 193.

488 Leopold Infeld, Quest: The Evolution of a Scientist (New York, 1941), p. 255.

489 Albert Einstein and Leopold Infeld, The Evolution of Physics (London, 1938), p. 33.

490 Ibid, p. 4.

491 Einstein, 'Nachruf auf Paul Ehrenfest'

('Obituary for Paul Ehrenfest') (1934); *Out of My Later Years* (1950), p. 238.

492 Richard Rhodes, *The Making of the Atomic Bomb* (Harmondsworth, 1988), p. 263.

493 Moszkowski (1972), p. 24.

494 Brian (1996), p. 271.

495 Nathan and Norden (1960), p. 291; Rhodes (1988), p. 305.

496 Rotblat (1980), p. 108.

497 Rhodes (1988), p. 314.

498 Einstein in conversation with Linus Pauling, 11 November 1954; Brian (1996), p. 420.

499 Einstein to Otto Hahn, 28 January 1949; Fölsing (1998), p. 728.

500 Einstein and Raymond Swing, 'Einstein on the Atomic Bomb', *Atlantic Monthly* (November 1945), pp. 347–52; from Brian (1996), p. 344.

501 Einstein speaking in New York, December 1945; French (1979), p. 193.

502 Einstein speaking in New York, December 1945; ibid, p. 193.

503 Rotblat (1980), p. 115.

504 Einstein's FBI file is now available on the Internet. This statement appears on the first page at http://foia.fbi.gov/einstein.htm. All quotations are from documents available at this address.

505 United States Government Confidential Memorandum from Mr D M Ladd to The Director, Subject: Professor Albert Einstein, 15 February 1950, pp. 1–2.

506 United States Government Confidential Memorandum from V P Keay to Mr H B Fletcher, Subject: Professor Albert Einstein, 13 February 1950, p. 9.

507 Einstein to Margarita Konenkova, 27 November 1945; Calaprice (2000), p. 87.

508 Einstein to Margarita Konenkova, n.d.; *The Times*, 2 June 1998, p. 13.

509 Einstein in *New York World Telegram*, 19 September 1933; Pais (1994), p. 194.

510 *New York Times*, 14 June 1953; ibid, p. 238.

511 Brian (1996), p. 301.

512 Einstein to Erwin Schrödinger, 27 January 1947; Fölsing (1998), p. 730.

513 Brian (1996), p. 373.

514 Einstein to Karl Zürcher, 29 July 1947; Highfield and Carter (1993), p. 252.

515 Maria Grendelmeier, interview, August 1992; ibid, p. 253.

516 Einstein to Carl Seelig, 4 January 1954; ibid, p. 257.

517 Seelig to Einstein, 22 March 1952; ibid, p. 257.

518 Einstein to Hans Albert, 1 May 1954; ibid, p. 258.

519 Einstein to Lina Kocherthaler, 27 July 1951; Fölsing (1998), p. 731.

520 Conversation between David Ben-Gurion and Yitzak Navon; in Yitzak Navon, 'On Einstein and the Presidency of Israel', *Albert Einstein: Historical and Cultural Perspectives. The Centennial Symposium in Jerusalem*, eds Gerald Holton and Yehuda Elkana (Princeton, 1982), p. 294.

521 Conversation between David Ben-Gurion and Yitzak Navon; in Navon (1982), p. 295.

522 Einstein to Abba Eban, 18 November 1952; Fölsing (1998), p. 733.

523 Habicht and Solovine to Einstein, 12 March 1953; Hoffmann (1975), pp. 243–4.

524 Einstein to Habicht and Solovine, 3 April 1953; ibid, p. 244.

525 Einstein to Max von Laue, 23 March 1934; Fölsing (1998), p. 694.

526 March 1955; Abraham Pais, 'Einstein, Newton, and Success', in French (1979), p. 37.

527 Einstein to Vero and Bice Besso, 21 March 1955; Fölsing (1998), p. 429.

528 Einstein to Mileva, 27 March 1901; Renn and Schulmann (1992), p. 39.

529 Helen Dukas to Abraham Pais, 30 April 1955; Pais (1982), p. 477.

530 French (1979), p. 304.

531 Dr Henry Adams, interview, 23 June 1995; Brian (1996), p. 439.

532 Roland Barthes, *Mythologies* (London, 1972), p. 69.

533 Graham Farmelo, 'Foreword', *It Must Be Beautiful: Great Equations of Modern Science*, ed Graham Farmelo (London, 2002), p. xiii.

534 Einstein, 'What I believe' (1930); French (1979), p. 304.

535 Armin Hermann, *Albert Einstein* (Munich, 1994), p. 158; Calaprice (2000), p. 157.

536 Michael Harwood, 'The Universe and Dr Hawking', in *New York Times Magazine*, 23 January 1983, p. 56.

Chronology

Year	Age	Life
1879		14 March: Albert Einstein born in Ulm, Germany; parents: Hermann Einstein (1847–1902) and Pauline Einstein, née Koch (1858–1920).
1880		The Einstein family move to 3 Müllerstrasse, Munich.
1881	2	18 November: Maria (Maja) Einstein born.
1883–4		Einstein's *wonder* at a compass given to him by his father. Private tuition at home.
1885	6	31 March: family moves to 14 Rengerweg (later renamed Adlzreiterstrasse), Sendling district. October: Einstein enters Petersschule on Blumenstrasse, a Catholic primary school. Starts violin lessons (continue till age of 14).
1888	9	October: passes the entry examinations for Luitpold Gymnasium, Munich. Receives religious instruction at the school from Heinrich Friedmann.
1889	10	Meets 21-year-old medical student Max Talmud who over the next five years introduces Einstein to some key scientific and philosophical texts.
1891	12	Einstein experiences a *second wonder* – the *holy little book of geometry*.
1894	15	June: Einstein family firm goes into liquidation and they move to Via Berchet 2, Milan. Einstein remains in Munich until 29 December when he withdraws from school and joins his family in Italy.
1895	16	Family moves to Via Foscolo 11 in nearby Pavia and establishes an electrotechnical factory. They sell it a year later and move back to Milan. Einstein writes his first scientific essay, 'On the Investigation of the State of the Ether in a Magnetic Field', in the summer and sends it to his uncle, Caesar Koch. 8 October: Einstein fails entry examination to the Swiss Polytechnic in Zurich. 26 October: enrolls in the Technical School of the Aarau Cantonal School; lives in Aarau, Switzerland with the family of Jost Winteler.
1896	17	28 January: released from Württemberg (and hence German) citizenship. Falls in love with Marie Winteler. September: Einstein passes his school leaving exams with flying colours. October: begins studies at the Polytechnic. Lives at 4 Unionstrasse.

Year	History	Culture
1879	Dual alliance between Germany and Austria-Hungary. Zulu War in Africa. War of the Pacific (until 1883).	Henrik Ibsen, *A Doll's House*. The term 'anti-Semitism' coined by Wilhelm Marr.
1880	William Gladstone becomes British prime minister. First Boer War (until 1881).	Dostoevsky, *The Brothers Karamazov*. Tchaikovsky, *1812 Overture*.
1881	Tsar Alexander II assassinated. Jewish pogroms in eastern Europe. The Mahdi Holy War begins in Sudan (until 1898).	Natural History Museum, London, opened. Henry James, *Portrait of a Lady*.
1883	Jewish immigration to Palestine (Rothschild Colonies). World's first skyscraper in Chicago.	Friedrich Nietzsche, *Thus Spake Zarathustra*. R L Stevenson, *Treasure Island*.
1885	Lord Salisbury becomes British prime minister. Canadian Pacific railway completed. British occupy Burma. Gold discovered in Transvaal.	Niels Bohr born. Emile Zola, *Germinal*.
1888	William II becomes German emperor. French establish Indo-China.	Rimsky-Korsakov, *Scheherezade*. *Financial Times*, London, first published.
1889	Second Socialist International. Great London dock strike. Birth of Adolf Hitler.	Verdi, *Falstaff*. First international congress of psychology in Paris. Eiffel Tower is finally completed.
1891	The United States of Brazil formed. Building of Trans-Siberian railway begins.	Tchaikovsky, *The Nutcracker*. Wilde, *The Picture of Dorian Gray*.
1894	Armenian massacres by Turks. Japan declares war against China. French Jewish army officer Nicholas II becomes Russian tsar. Pullman strike in United States.	Rudyard Kipling, *The Jungle Book*. G B Shaw, *Arms and the Man*. Wilde, *A Woman of No Importance* and *Salome*.
1895	Japan gets Formosa, and a free hand in Korea. New Cuban revolution against the Spanish.	H G Wells, *The Time Machine*. Wilde, *The Importance of Being Earnest*. Guglielmo Marconi sends message over a mile by wireless. Sigmund Freud publishes first work on psychoanalysis. Lumière brothers show first moving pictures.
1896	Italian disaster at hands of Abyssinians. Gold discovered in the Klondike, Canada.	Hardy, *Jude the Obscure*. Puccini, *La Bohème*. Nobel Prizes established. Theodor Herzl, *Der Judenstaat*; foundation of Zionism.

143

Year	Age	Life
1897	18	Meets Michele Angelo Besso. October–April 1898: fellow student Mileva Marić attends lectures in Heidelberg.
1898	19	October: Einstein passes intermediate diploma exam. Moves to 87 Klosbachstrasse.
1899	20	March: reprimanded by Professor Pernet for poor attendance. 19 October: applies for Swiss citizenship. 9 November: moves back to 4 Unionstrasse.
1900	21	27 July: passes diploma and is qualified to teach mathematical subjects. Mileva fails. August: reveals plans to marry Mileva to his mother. October: returns to Zurich to work on doctorate, but fails to win an assistantship at the Poly. 13 December: submits his first scientific paper to the *Annalen der Physik*; published the following March.
1901	22	21 February: becomes Swiss citizen. 5 May: meets Mileva at Lake Como. 16 May–11 July: substitute teacher at the Technical School in Winterthur. In May Mileva tells him she is pregnant. September: tutor at Schaffhausen. November: submits doctoral dissertation to Zurich University; Mileva returns to her parents in Novi Sad. 18 December: applies for a position at the Swiss Patent Office in Bern.
1902	23	January: Lieserl is born. 11 February: Einstein withdraws his dissertation and moves to Bern, living at 32 Gerechtigkeitsgasse. Gives private lessons to Maurice Solovine, with whom he later founds the Olympia Academy. 30 April: submits second paper to the *Annalen*. 23 June: begins work as a Technical Expert Third Class at the Patent Office. Lives at 43A Thunstrasse. 10 October: Einstein's father dies, aged 55.
1903	24	6 January: marries Mileva in Bern. August: Mileva visits her parents, possibly to arrange adoption of Lieserl, who has fallen ill with scarlet fever.
1904	25	14 May: son Hans Albert born (*d.* 1973, Berkeley, California). 16 September: position at the patent office is made permanent.
1905	26	17 March: submits paper 'On a Heuristic Point of View Concerning the Production and Transformation of Light' to *Annalen*. 30 April: completes doctoral dissertation, 'A New Determination of Molecular Dimensions'. 11 May: the *Annalen* receives 'On the Motion of Small Particles Suspended in Liquids at Rest Required by the Molecular-Kinetic Theory of Heat'. 30 June: *Annalen* receives 'On the Electrodynamics of Moving Bodies', the special theory of relativity (published 26 September). 27 September: *Annalen* receives 'Does the Inertia of a Body Depend on its Energy Content?', the paper that forms the basis of $E=mc^2$. May: The Einsteins move from 49 Kramgasse to 28 Besenscheuerweg. In the summer, Einstein travels with Mileva and son to Belgrade and Novi Sad.

Year	History	Culture
1897	Greek-Turkish War. Hawaii annexed by USA. Great Gold Rush begins.	Bram Stoker, *Dracula*. J J Thomson discovers the electron.
1898	Spanish-American War: Spain loses Cuba, Puerto Rico, and the Philippines. Empress of Austria assassinated.	James, *The Turn of the Screw*. Wells, *The War of the Worlds*. Marie and Pierre Curie discover radium.
1899	Second Boer War (until 1901). Relief of Mafeking. In China, Boxer rebellion (until 1901).	Elgar, *Enigma Variations*. Aspirin introduced.
1900	Annexation of Orange Free State. Annexation of the Transvaal. Australian Commonwealth proclaimed.	Joseph Conrad, *Lord Jim*. Freud, *The Interpretation of Dreams*. Puccini, *Tosca*. Planck's quantum theory explaining black-body radiation. Mendel's laws of heredity 're-discovered'.
1901	Queen Victoria dies. Edward VII becomes king. US President William McKinley assassinated. Theodore Roosevelt becomes president. Trans-Siberian railway opens.	Anton Chekhov, *The Three Sisters*. Thomas Mann, *Buddenbrooks*. Shaw, *Man and Superman*. Enrico Fermi and Werner Heisenberg born.
1902	Anglo-Japanese alliance. Treaty of Vereeniging ends Boer War.	Conrad, *The Heart of Darkness*. Arthur Conan Doyle, *The Hound of the Baskervilles*. Debussy, *Pelléas et Mélisande*. French mathematician Henri Poincaré's *Science and Hypothesis* published. *Times Literary Supplement* first appears.
1903	Royal family of Serbia assassinated. Pogroms against Jews in Russia. Panama Canal Zone granted to USA.	James, *The Ambassadors*. Wilbur and Orville Wright fly first manned, powered aircraft.
1904	Russo-Japanese War begins. France and Britain sign Entente Cordiale.	J M Barrie, *Peter Pan*. Chekhov, *The Cherry Orchard*.
1905	3 January: Port Arthur falls to Japanese. 22 January: 'Bloody Sunday' massacre at St Petersburg. Treaty of Portsmouth (USA) ends Russo-Japanese War. Separation of Church and State in France. Norway separates itself from Sweden.	F T Marinetti, *Futurist Manifesto*. Richard Strauss, *Salome*. In London the Piccadilly and Bakerloo underground lines open.

Year	Age	Life
1906	27	Receives doctorate from University of Zurich. 1 April: promoted to Technical Expert Second Class. 9 November: completes the first paper written on the quantum theory of the solid state.
1907	28	Has the *happiest thought of my life*: the equivalence principle, which leads to the general theory of relativity. Max von Laue visits.
1908	29	24 February: becomes Privatdozent at Bern University. April: Jakob Laub, Einstein's first collaborator in physics, visits. Einstein designs a *little machine* for measuring minute voltages. 21 December: Maja receives a doctorate in Romance languages from Bern University.
1909	30	7 May: Einstein appointed Extraordinary Professor of Theoretical Physics at the University of Zurich. 6 July: resigns from patent office. 9 July: receives first honorary doctorate, from Geneva University. 21 September: lectures on radiation theory at the Congress of German Natural Scientists and Physicians. 2 October: nominated for a Nobel Prize in Physics. 15 October: moves to 12 Moussonstrasse, Zurich, and begins teaching. The Anna Meyer-Schmid affair sours relations with Mileva.
1910	31	March: Maja marries Paul Winteler. 21 April: Einstein proposed for a professorship at University of Prague. 28 July: second son born, Eduard (*d.* 1965, Zurich). October: finishes a paper on opalescence.
1911	32	6 January: appointed to the chair at the German University, Prague. The Einsteins leave Zurich at the end of March. June: Einstein realises that a total eclipse would enable his theory of the bending of light to be tested. November: delivers lecture on 'The Current State of the Problem of Specific Heat' to first Solvay Congress, Brussels.
1912	33	30 January: appointed Professor of Theoretical Physics at the Zurich Polytechnic (after 1911 the Swiss Federal Technical University). 15–22 April: visits Berlin and renews acquaintance with his cousin Elsa Löwenthal (née Einstein). 25 July: returns to Zurich. August: start of collaboration with Marcel Grossmann on mathematical aspects of the general theory of relativity.
1913	34	July: Max Planck and Walther Nernst visit and offer Einstein membership of the Prussian Academy of Sciences and a professorship without teaching obligations at Berlin University. December: formally accepts their offer and resigns his position at Zurich.
1914	35	April: Einstein arrives in Berlin. July: inaugural address to the Prussian Academy; at the end of the month he and Mileva separate; she returns with the boys to Zurich. November: shocked by the outbreak of war, Einstein signs Georg Nicolai's anti-war 'Manifesto to Europeans'.

Year	History	Culture
1906	General Strike in Russia. 18 April: San Francisco destroyed by earthquake. Liberal 'landslide' majority in Britain.	Physicist Ludwig Boltzmann dies. Norwegian dramatist Henrik Ibsen dies.
1907	New Zealand becomes a dominion. Anglo-Russian Entente.	R M Rilke, *New Poems*. Pablo Picasso's *Les Demoiselles d'Avignon*.
1908	Annexation of Congo by Belgium. Young Turk revolution. Annexation of Bosnia and Herzegovina by Austria.	E M Forster, *A Room with a View*. Hermann Minkowski formulates the idea of the four-dimensional space-time continuum. Henri Matisse coins the term 'Cubism'.
1909	Union of South Africa formed. United States supports revolution in Nicaragua. Britain begins oil drilling in Iran.	Strauss, *Elektra*. Sergei Diaghilev forms Ballets Russes. French aviator Louis Blériot makes first cross-Channel flight in a monoplane. Henry Ford produces Model T chassis, the beginnings of cheap motorcars. Frederick Soddy, *The Interpretation of Radium*.
1910	George V becomes king.	Forster, *Howards End*. Stravinsky, *The Firebird*. London's first Post-Impressionist exhibition.
1911	Rail strike in Britain. Tripoli taken from Turkey by Italy. Chinese Revolution against imperial dynasties. 14 December: Norwegian explorer Roald Amundsen reaches South Pole.	Conrad, *Under Western Eyes*. Ernest Rutherford proposes a nuclear model of the atom. First Solvay Congress of physicists. Escalators first introduced, at Earls Court Station.
1912	China becomes a republic under Sun Yat Sen. Scott's expedition reaches the South Pole, only to find Amundsen has beaten them. *Titanic* strikes an iceberg and sinks: 1,513 lives are lost. Outbreak of Balkan Wars. African National Congress formed.	Henri Poincaré dies. Wassily Kandinsky, *On the Spiritual in Art*. Futurist exhibition in Paris. Stainless steel invented.
1913	Treaty of Bucharest: most of Turkey-in-Europe divided among Balkan states. Woodrow Wilson becomes US president.	Thomas Mann, *Death in Venice*. Marcel Proust, *A la recherche du temps perdu* (until 1927). Stravinsky, *The Rite of Spring*.
1914	First World War begins. Austria-Hungary declares war on Serbia. Germany declares war on Russia. Germany declares war on France. Germany invades Belgium: Britain declares war on Germany. Britain declares war on Austria-Hungary. Japan declares war on Germany. Britain declares war on Turkey.	James Joyce, *Dubliners*. Hermann Hesse, *Rosshalde*. Wyndham Lewis founds Vorticist movement.

Year	Age	Life
1915	36	June: stays with David Hilbert in Göttingen and lectures on general theory of relativity. 4–25 November: four lectures to Prussian Academy outlining completed general theory of relativity.
1916	37	20 March: completes 'The Foundations of the General Theory of Relativity', his first systematic account of the theory; published in the *Annalen* and as a book. 5 May: succeeds Planck as president of German Physical Society. July: after working on gravitational waves he returns to quantum theory. Mileva is hospitalised. December: Einstein completes *Relativity: The Special and the General Theory. A Popular Exposition.*
1917	38	Einstein suffers a physical collapse and has to be cared for by Elsa. February: writes first paper on cosmology and introduces the cosmological constant.
1919	40	January: lectures in Zurich. 14 February: divorces Mileva. 2 June: marries Elsa. 22 September: learns (via telegram from Lorentz) that the two British expeditions to observe the solar eclipse have confirmed his prediction about the bending of light by the gravitational field of the sun. 6 November: formal announcement of this in London and reported around the world the following day. His friend Kurt Blumenfeld encourages his interest in Zionism.
1920	41	February: Pauline Einstein dies. August: Einstein attends two anti-relativity lectures at the Berlin Philharmonic Hall and publishes an angry newspaper article condemning his opponents. 23 September: argues with Philipp Lenard at the conference of the Society of German Natural Scientists and Physicians.
1921	42	1 April–30 May: first visit to USA. June: returns via England, where he lectures at Manchester and London.
1922	43	January: first paper on unified field theory. April: becomes a member of the League of Nations Commission for Intellectual Cooperation. 8 October: departs for the Far East; visits Colombo, Singapore, Hong Kong, Shanghai, and Japan. 8 November: awarded the 1921 Nobel Prize.
1923	44	2 February: arrives in Palestine after returning from Japan. 11 July: Nobel lecture in Göteborg, Sweden.
1923–4		Relationship with Betty Neumann.
1924	45	The Einstein Tower, an observatory in Potsdam, is opened. Ilse Einstein marries Rudolf Kaiser.
1924–5		Collaborates with Satyendra Nath Bose and discovers the state of matter known as the Bose-Einstein condensate.
1927	48	October: engages in intense debates about quantum mechanics at the Solvay Congress. Hans Albert marries Frieda Knecht.

Year	History	Culture
1915	22 May: Italy declares war on Austria. 26 May: British coalition government forms under Asquith. 28 November: Serbia conquered by Austria and Bulgaria.	Franz Kafka, 'Metamorphosis'. D H Lawrence, *The Rainbow*. Alfred Wegener outlines geological theory of plate tectonics.
1916	24 April: Easter Rising in Ireland. 1 July–13 November: Battle of the Somme (British losses: 420,000). 6 December: David Lloyd George forms War Cabinet.	G B Shaw, *Pygmalion*. Dada movement launched in Zurich with Cabaret Voltaire. Ernst Mach dies.
1917	Russia proclaimed a republic. Bolshevik Revolution. Balfour declaration recognises Palestine as 'a national home' for the Jews.	T S Eliot, *Prufrock*. W B Yeats, *The Wild Swans at Coole*. First recordings of New Orleans jazz.
1919	Spartacist revolt in Berlin. First direct flight across the Atlantic by Alcock and Brown. Treaty of Peace with Germany signed at Versailles. Treaty of St Germain: break-up of Austrian Empire. Prohibition begins in the United States. Irish Civil War (until 1921).	Bauhaus school of art founded by Walter Gropius, Weimar, Germany. United Artists formed with Charlie Chaplin, Mary Pickford, Douglas Fairbanks and D W Griffith as partners.
1920	First meeting of League of Nations. 10 August: Ottoman Empire broken up. 14 October: degrees first open to women at Oxford University. Irish Republican Army forms.	Edith Wharton, *The Age of Innocence*. A N Whitehead, *The Concept of Nature*.
1921	Irish Free State set up by peace treaty with Britain. Mao Ze Dong helps found the Chinese Communist Party.	Luigi Pirandello, *Six Characters in Search of an Author*. BBC founded. Chaplin's *The Kid*.
1922	Walther Rathenau assassinated. Heavy fighting in Dublin, the Four Courts blown up. Defeat of Greek armies by the Turks. Mussolini's Fascist 'March on Rome'. USSR formed.	T S Eliot, *The Waste Land*. Joyce, *Ulysses*. F W Murnau's *Nosferatu*. Ludwig Wittgenstein, *Tractatus Logico-Philosophicus*. Bohr wins Nobel Prize for physics.
1923	Hitler's Munich Putsch fails. 1 September: earthquake in Japan, Tokyo in ruins. Turkish republic proclaimed with Kemal Pasha as first president.	Rilke, *Sonnets to Orpheus* and *Duino Elegies*. George Gershwin, *Rhapsody in Blue*. Le Corbusier, *Towards a New Architecture*.
1924	Lenin dies. First Labour Ministry in Britain (lasts nine months). George II of Greece deposed and a republic declared.	Forster, *A Passage to India*.
1925	Pact of Locarno.	F Scott Fitzgerald, *The Great Gatsby*. Adolf Hitler, *Mein Kampf*.
1927	Lindbergh makes non-stop solo Atlantic flight. Stalin comes to power in USSR.	Virginia Woolf, *To The Lighthouse*. Martin Heidegger, *Being and Time*.

Year	Age	Life
1928	49	Einstein collapses in Davos; confined to bed for four months, but continues to work on his unified field theory. April: Helen Dukas (*d.* 1982) becomes Einstein's secretary.
1929	50	Visits the Belgian royal family. The Einsteins build a summer home at Caputh. Einstein's unified field theory.
1930	51	First grandchild, Bernhard, born to Frieda and Hans Albert; step-daughter Margot (*d.* 1986) marries Dmitri Marianoff (marriage ended in divorce). Eduard develops schizophrenia. December: Einstein begins a visiting professorship at California Institute of Technology in Pasadena.
1931	52	Einstein finally rejects the cosmological constant as unnecessary. May: offered research fellowship at Christ Church College, Oxford. 30 December–4 March 1932 at Caltech.
1932	53	August: appointed to the new Institute for Advanced Study in Princeton, starting October 1933. 10 December: Einstein and Elsa depart for Caltech, intending to return to Caputh in March the following year.
1933	54	March: Einstein's Caputh home is searched by Nazis; at the end of the month he returns to Europe, staying in Belgium. He resigns from the Prussian Academy. An exchange of letters between Einstein and Freud is published as *Why War?* Visits Eduard and Mileva for the last time. 17 October: arrives in New York and goes straight to Princeton. Rents a house at 2 Library Place.
1934	55	Stepdaughter Ilse Kayser-Einstein dies in Paris, aged 37. Margot and Dimitri come to Princeton.
1935	56	May: travels to Bermuda to apply for permanent residency in America. It is the last time he leaves America. August: the Einsteins and Dukas move to 112 Mercer Street, his final home. Einstein receives the Franklin medal.
1936	57	Hans Albert receives doctorate from the Polytechnic in Zurich. 7 September: Marcel Grossmann dies. 20 December: Elsa dies aged 60.
1937	58	Hans Albert emigrates to America with his family. Collaboration with Leopold Infeld on *The Evolution of Physics*.
1939	60	Maja comes to live with her brother in Princeton. 2 August: Einstein signs the letter to President Roosevelt warning of the threat posed by atomic weapons.

Year	History	Culture
1928	23 April: earthquake in Greece, Corinth destroyed. British women enfranchised on same basis as men.	Lawrence, *Lady Chatterley's Lover*. Ravel, *Boléro*. First Mickey Mouse cartoon.
1929	Stock market crash on Wall Street and beginning of the Depression.	Faulkner, *The Sound and the Fury*. Graves, *Goodbye to All That*.
1930	Mahatma Gandhi leads Salt March in India.	W H Auden, *Poems*. Evelyn Waugh, *Vile Bodies*. Paul Dirac, *The Principles of Quantum Mechanics*. Marlene Dietrich appears in *The Blue Angel*.
1931	Great floods in China. King Alfonso XIII flees and a Spanish republic formed. New Zealand becomes independent.	Empire State Building completed. Boris Karloff in *Frankenstein*. Bela Lugosi in *Dracula*.
1932	Manchuria becomes Japanese puppet state. Sydney Harbour Bridge opened. Iraq and Saudi Arabia become independent.	Aldous Huxley, *Brave New World*. James Chadwick discovers the neutron. Heisenberg wins Nobel Prize. Fritz Lang's *M*.
1933	Hitler appointed Chancellor. Civil liberties are suspended by the Nazis. First concentration camp is opened at Dachau. 'The Law for the Restoration of the Professional Civil Service' is used to remove Jews from government posts. F D Roosevelt becomes US president.	André Malraux, *La Condition Humaine*. Gertrude Stein, *The Autobiography of Alice B Toklas*. Wells, *The Shape of Things to Come*. Books by Jews and left-wing writers are burnt in Nazi Germany.
1934	Hitler consolidates his power by murdering rivals. Long March in China.	Agatha Christie, *Murder on the Orient Express*.
1935	3 October: war begins between Italy and Abyssinia. Nuremberg Laws in Germany. The Philippines becomes self-governing. Italy invades Ethiopia.	Christopher Isherwood, *Mr Norris Changes Trains*. George Orwell, *A Clergyman's Daughter*. Marx Brothers' *A Night at the Opera*.
1936	Accession of Edward VIII. Germany occupies the Rhineland. Civil war breaks out in Spain. Edward VIII abdicates. Succession of George VI. Anti-Comintern Pact between Japan and Germany.	Cyril Connolly, *The Rock Pool*. John Maynard Keynes, *The General Theory of Employment, Interest and Money*. Olympic Games held in Berlin. Chaplin's *Modern Times*.
1937	Nanjing massacre. Arab-Jewish conflict in Palestine.	John Steinbeck, *Of Mice and Men*. Picasso, *Guernica*.
1939	The Second World War begins. Germany invades Poland. Britain and France declare war. Russian troops on Polish border. Stalin and Hitler sign Nazi-Soviet pact in Moscow approving of partition of Poland. Finland attacked by Russia. Francisco Franco becomes dictator in Spain.	John Steinbeck, *The Grapes of Wrath*. Sigmund Freud dies. The first nylon stockings marketed. John Ford's *Stagecoach* (with John Wayne). David O Selznick's *Gone with the Wind* (with Vivien Leigh and Clark Gable). Judy Garland appears in *The Wizard of Oz*.

1940	61	Einstein becomes an American citizen.
1943	64	Einstein becomes a consultant with the Research and Development Division of the US Navy Bureau of Ordnance for a fee of $25 a day.
1944	65	A handwritten copy of Einstein's special relativity paper is auctioned for $6 million as a contribution to the war effort.
1945	66	10 December: at a speech in New York Einstein declares *The war is won, but the peace is not*. He begins campaigning for world government as a way of ensuring peace.
1946	67	Maja is bedridden after a stroke.
1947	68	Hans Albert becomes a professor of hydraulic engineering at the University of California at Berkeley.
1948	69	4 August: Mileva dies in Zurich aged 73. December: after an operation on Einstein, surgeons discover an aneurysm of the abdominal aorta.
1950	71	18 March: Einstein draws up a will in which he bequeaths his papers to the Hebrew University and his violin to his grandson, Bernhard.
1951	72	25 June: Maja dies.
1952	73	November: Einstein is offered the presidency of Israel, but declines.
1955	76	15 March: Michele Besso dies in Geneva, aged 82. 11 April: Einstein's last signed letter is to Bertrand Russell, agreeing to add his name to a manifesto calling all nations to renounce nuclear weapons. 13 April: rupture of aortic aneurysm. 15 April: admitted to Princeton hospital. 18 April: Einstein dies. His body is cremated the same day and his ashes scattered at a secret location.

Year	History	Culture
1940	German invasion of Europe continues. Evacuation of British from Dunkirk. Italy declares war on Britain and France. Germans capture Paris. Battle of Britain. Leon Trotsky assassinated in Mexico.	Graham Greene, *The Power and the Glory*. Hemingway, *For Whom the Bell Tolls*. Arthur Koestler, *Darkness at Noon*. Chaplin's *The Great Dictator*. Disney's *Fantasia*.
1943	German army outside Stalingrad surrender. Mussolini overthrown. Fascist Party in Italy dissolved. Teheran Conference.	T S Eliot, *Four Quartets*. Ingrid Bergman and Humphrey Bogart in *Casablanca*.
1944	D-Day, invasion of Europe. 'Bomb plot' on Hitler's life. Paris liberated.	J L Borges, *Fictions*. Eisenstein's *Ivan the Terrible*.
1945	Dresden bombed. Mussolini murdered. German and Italian armies in Italy surrender. Hitler commits suicide. German forces surrender. VE Day, end of WWII. Atomic bombs destroy Hiroshima and Nagasaki. VJ Day.	Orwell, *Animal Farm*. Hesse, *The Glass Bead Game*. Benjamin Britten, *Peter Grimes*. Karl Popper, *The Open Society and Its Enemies*. Frank Lloyd Wright designs Guggenheim Museum.
1946	Winston Churchill's 'Iron Curtain' speech. League of Nations wound up. Nuremberg sentences executed: Goering commits suicide. UN formed.	Dylan Thomas, *Deaths and Entrances*. Cocteau's *La belle et la bête*.
1947	'Marshall Plan' inaugurated. India and Pakistan independent after partition.	Tennessee Williams, *A Streetcar Named Desire*.
1948	Gandhi assassinated. State of Israel proclaimed. Harry S Truman elected as US president. UN adopts Declaration of Human Rights.	Graves, *The White Goddess*. Greene, *The Heart of the Matter*. Norman Mailer, *The Naked and the Dead*.
1950	Indian republic proclaimed. USSR-China alliance signed. North Korea invades South Korea. US offensive in Korea. Chinese offensive into North Korea.	T S Eliot, *The Cocktail Party*. Alan Turing explores the possibility of thinking machines in 'Computing Machines and Intelligence'.
1951	Festival of Britain. Korean ceasefire talks. Pakistan's Prime Minister Ali Khan assassinated. British troops seize Suez Canal Zone. Churchill becomes PM again.	J D Salinger, *The Catcher in the Rye*. Electric power produced from atomic energy in Idaho, USA. Orson Welles' *Othello*.
1952	George VI dies. Accession of Elizabeth II. US air attacks on North Korea. West Germany independent again. Eisenhower wins US presidential elections. First hydrogen bomb exploded by America.	Samuel Beckett, *En attendant Godot*. Hemingway, *The Old Man and the Sea*. Steinbeck, *East of Eden*. Gary Cooper and Grace Kelly in *High Noon*.
1955	Churchill resigns: Sir Anthony Eden becomes British PM. Vietnam civil war. Vietnam declared independent republic. Warsaw Pact formed.	Vladimir Nabokov, *Lolita*. Tolkein, *The Lord of the Rings*. Waugh, *Officers and Gentlemen*. First broadcast of ITV in Britain. German première of Bertolt Brecht's play *The Life of Galileo*.

List of Works

ABBREVIATIONS

AP = Annalen der Physik

SB = Königlich Preußische Akademie der Wissenschaften (Berlin) *Sitzungsberichte*

1901 'Folgerungen aus den Capillaritätserscheinungen' ('Conclusions Drawn from the Phenomena of Capillarity'), *AP* 4 (1901), pp. 513–23.

1902 'Über die thermodynamische Theorie der Potentialdifferenz zwischen Metallen and vollständig dissociirten Lösungen ihrer Salze und über eine elektrische Methode zur Erforschung der Molecularkräfte' ('On the Thermodynamic Theory of the Difference in Potentials between Metals and Fully Dissociated Solutions of Their Salts and on an Electrical Method for Investigating Molecular Forces'), *AP* 8 (1902), pp. 798–814.

'Kinetische Theorie des Wärmegleichgewichtes und des zweiten Hauptsatzes der Thermodynamik' ('Kinetic Theory of the Thermal Equilibrium and of the Second Law of Thermodynamics'), *AP* 9 (1902), pp. 417–33.

1903 'Eine Theorie der Grundlagen der Thermodynamik' ('A Theory of the Foundations of Thermodynamics'), *AP* 11 (1903), pp. 170–87.

1904 'Zur allgemeinen molekularen Theorie der Wärme' ('On the General Molecular Theory of Heat'), *AP* 14 (1904), pp. 354–62.

1905 'Über einen die Erzeugung und Verwandlung des Lichtes betreffenden heuristischen Gesichtspunkt' ('On a Heuristic Point of View Concerning the Production and Transformation of Light'), *AP* 17 (1905), pp. 132–48.

Eine neue Bestimmung der Moleküldimensionen (A New Determination of Molecular Dimensions), doctoral thesis, completed 30 April 1905, printed by K J Wyss, Bern, 1906. (Also in *AP* 19 (1906), pp. 289–305.)

'Über die von der molekularkinetischen Theorie der Wärme geforderte Bewegung von in ruhenden Flüssigkeiten suspendierten Teilchen' ('On the Motion of Small Particles Suspended in Liquids at Rest Required by the Molecular-Kinetic Theory of Heat'), *AP* 17 (1905), pp. 549–60.

'Zur Elektrodynamik bewegter Körper' ('On the Electrodynamics of Moving Bodies'), *AP* 17 (1905), pp. 891–921.

'Ist die Trägheit eines Körpers von seinem Energieinhalt abhängig?' ('Does the Inertia of a Body Depend on its Energy Content?'), *AP* 18 (1905), pp. 639–41.

1906 'Zur Theorie der Lichterzeugung und Lichtabsorption' ('On the Theory of Light Production and Light Absorption'), *AP* 20 (1906), pp. 199–206.

1907 'Die Plancksche Theorie der Strahlung und die Theorie der spezifischen Wärme' ('Planck's Theory of Radiation and the Theory of Specific Heat'), *AP* 22 (1907), pp. 180–90.

'Über die Gültigkeitsgrenze des Satzes vom thermodynamischen Gleichgewicht und über die Möglichkeit einer neuen Bestimmung der Elementarquanta' ('On the Limit of Validity of the Law of Thermodynamic Equilibrium and on the Possibility of a New Determination of the Elementary Quanta'), *AP* 22 (1907), pp. 569–72.

1909 'Über die Entwickelung unserer Anschauungen über das Wesen und die Konstitution der Strahlung' ('On the Development of our Views Concerning the Nature and Constitution of Radiation'), lecture 21 September 1909; *Deutsche Physikalische Gesellschaft. Verhandlungen 7* (1909), pp. 482–500.

1910 'Theorie der Opaleszenz von homogenen Flüssigkeiten und Flüssigkeitsgemischen in der Nähe des kritischen Zustandes' ('Theory of Opalescence of Homogeneous Fluids and Liquid Mixtures near the Critical State'), *AP* 33 (1910), pp. 1275–98.

1911 'Über den Einfluß der Schwerkraft auf die Ausbreitung des Lichtes' ('On the Influence of Gravitation on the Propagation of Light'), *AP* 35 (1911), pp. 898–908.

1912 'Lichgeschwindigkeit und Statik des Gravitationsfeldes' ('The Speed of Light and the Statics of the Gravitational Field'), *AP* 38 (1912), pp. 443–58.

'Zur Theorie des statischen des Gravitationsfeldes' ('On the Theory of the Static Gravitational Field'), *AP* 38 (1912), pp. 443–58.

1913 *Entwurf einer verallgemeinerten Relativitätstheorie und einer Theorie der Gravitation* (Outline of a Generalized Theory of Relativity and of a Theory of Gravitation), I. Physical Part by Albert Einstein, II. Mathematical Part by Marcel Grossmann (Leipzig, 1913).

1914 'Vom Relativitäts-Prinzip' ('On the Principle of Relativity'), *Vossische Zeitung*, 26 April 1914, pp. 33–4. Einstein's first newspaper article.

Inaugural Lecture to the Prussian Academy, 2 July 1914, *SB* (1914), pp. 739–42.

1915 'Erklärung der Perihelbewegung des Merkur aus der allgemeinen Relativitätstheorie' ('Explanation of the Perhelion Motion of Mercury from the General Theory of Relativity'), *SB* (1915), pp. 831–9.

1916 'Die Grundlage der allgemeinen Relativitätstheorie' ('The Foundation of the General Theory of Relativity'), *AP* 49 (1916), pp. 769–822. Later published as a book (Leipzig, 1916).

'Zur Quantentheorie der Strahlung' ('On the Quantum Theory of Radiation'), *Physikalische Gesellschaft Zürich. Mitteilungen* 18 (1916), pp. 47–62.

1917 'Kosmologische Betrachtungen zur allgemeinen Relativitätstheorie' ('Cosmological Considerations in the General Theory of Relativity'), *SB* (1917), pp. 142–52.

Über die spezielle und die allgemeine Relitivitätstheorie. (Gemeinverständlich.) (Braunschweig); trans (by Robert W Lawson) *Relativity: The Special and the General Theory. A Popular Exposition* (London, 1920).

1918 'Über Gravitationswellen' ('On Gravitational Waves'), *SB* (1918), pp. 154–67.

1919 'Einstein on His Theory: Time, Space, and Gravitation', *The Times*, 28 November 1919, pp 13–14.

1920 'Meine Antwort. Über die anti-relativitätstheoretische Gmbh' ('My Response. On the Anti-Relativity Company'), *Berliner Tageblatt*, 27 August 1920, pp. 1–2.

1921 'A Brief Outline of the Development of the Theory of Relativity', *Nature* 106 (1921), pp. 782–4.

Vier Vorlesungen über Relativitätstheorie, gehalten im Mai 1921 an der Universität Princeton (Braunschweig, 1922); *The Meaning of Relativity: Four Lectures Delivered at Princeton University, May 1921*, trans. by E P Adams (Princeton, 1922); Einstein's first book published in America, subsequently revised by Einstein through five editions.

1922 'In Memoriam Walther Rathenau', *Neue Rundschau* 33 (1922), pp. 815–16.

1923 *Grundgedanken und Probleme zur Relativitätstheorie* (Fundamental Ideas and Problems of the Theory of Relativity), Nobel lecture, Göteborg 11 June 1923 (Stockholm, 1923), 10 pp.

'Beweis für die Nichtexistenz eines überall regulären zentrisch symmetrischen Feldes nach der Feldtheorie von Kaluza' ('Proof of the Nonexistence of a Universally Regular Centrally Symmetrical

Field According to Kaluza's Field Theory'), with Jakob Grommer, *Scripta Mathematica et Physica*, Hebrew University, Jerusalem, 1.7 (1923). First paper on unified field theory.

1924 'Quantentheorie des einatomigen idealen Gases' ('Quantum Theory of Single-Atom Ideal Gases'), *SB* (1924), pp. 261–7.

1925 'Quantentheorie des einatomigen idealen Gases' ('Quantum Theory of Single-Atom Ideal Gases'), *SB* (1925), pp. 3–14 and 18–25.

1927 'Isaac Newton', *Manchester Guardian*, 10 March 1927.

1929 'Zur einheitlichen Feldtheorie' ('On the Unified Field Theory'), *SB* (1929), pp. 2–7.

'The New Field Theory', *New York Times*, 3 February 1929; *The Times* (London), 4 February 1929.

'Space-Time', *Encyclopaedia Britannica*, 14th ed., Vol 21, 1929, pp. 105–8.

1930 *About Zionism: Speeches and Letters*, ed and trans Leon Simon (London).

'Théorie unitaire du champ physique' ('Unified Physical Field Theory'), *Annales de l'Institut Henri Poincaré* 1 (1930), pp. 1–24.

'Religion und Wissenschaft' ('Religion and Science'), *New York Times*, 9 November 1930; *Berliner Tageblatt*, 11 November 1930.

'Concept of Space', *Nature*, 125 (1930), pp. 897–98.

1931 'Zum kosmologischen Problem der Allgemeinen Relativitätstheorie' ('On the Cosmological Problem of the General Theory of Relativity'), *SB* (1931), pp. 235–37.

1932 'On the Relation Between the Expansion and the Mean Density of the Universe', with Willem de Sitter, *Proceedings of the National Academy of Science*, 18 (1932), pp. 213–14.

1933 *Why War?*, with Sigmund Freud (Paris).

On the Methods of Theoretical Physics, Spence Lecture, Oxford University, 10 June 1933 (Oxford).

Origins of the General Theory of Relativity, Gibson Lecture, Glasgow University, 20 June 1933, *Glasgow University Publications* No 20.

1934 *Mein Weltbild* (Amsterdam); trans (by Alan Harris) *The World as I See It* (New York).

'Nachruf auf Paul Ehrenfest' ('Obituary for Paul Ehrenfest'), *Almanak van het Leidensche Studentencorps* (1934). Also in *Out of My Later Years*.

1935 'Can Quantum-Mechanical Description Be Considered Complete?' with B Podolsky and N Rosen, *Physical Review* 47 (1935), pp. 777–80.

1936 'Lens-like Action of a Star by Deviation of Light in the Gravitational field', *Science* 84 (1936), pp. 506–7.

1938 *The Evolution of Physics: The Growth of Ideas from Early Concepts to Relativity and Quanta*, with Leopold Infeld (New York).

1945 'Influence of the Expansion of Space on the Gravitation Fields Surrounding the Individual Stars', with Ernst G Straus, *Review of Modern Physics* 17 (1945), pp. 120–24.

1946 'E=mc²: The Most Urgent Problem of Our Time', *Science Illustrated* 1 (April 1946), pp. 16–17

1947 'An Open Letter to the General Assembly of the United Nations, on "the Way to break the Vicious Circle,"' *United Nations World* 1 (Oct 1947), pp. 13–4

1948 'A Plea for International Understanding', *Bulletin of the Atomic Scientists* 4 (1948), p. 1.

'Quantenmechanik und Wirklichkeit' ('Quantum Mechanics and Reality'), *Dialectica* 2 (1948), pp. 320–24.

1949 'Autobiographical Notes', *Albert Einstein: Philosopher-Scientist*, ed Paul Arthur Schilpp (Evanston, Ill)

'Why Socialism?', *Monthly Review* 1 (1949), pp. 9–15.

1950 *Out of My Later Years* (New York).

'On the Generalized Theory of Gravitation', *Scientific American* 82 (April 1950), pp. 13–17.

1954 *Ideas and Opinions*, trans Sonja Bargmann (New York).

'Algebraic Properties of the Field in the Relativistic Theory of the Asymmetric Field' (with Bruria Kaufmann, Einstein's last assistant) *Annals of Mathematics* 59 (1954), pp. 230–44.

1956 'Autobiographische Skizze' ('Autobiographical Sketch'), *Helle Zeit–Dunkle Zeit: In Memoriam Albert Einstein*, ed Carl Seelig (Zurich), pp. 9–10.

Further Reading

There are many popular editions of Einstein's writings. His two main attempts at popularising his ideas are *Relativity: The Special and the General Theory. A Popular Exposition*, translated by Robert W Lawson (London, 1920), and (with Leopold Infeld) *The Evolution of Physics: The Growth of Ideas from Early Concepts to Relativity and Quanta* (New York, 1938). Both are still available in various editions and are well worth reading, although for the reader with little knowledge of physics they may now seem somewhat complex.

Of Einstein's non-scientific writings *The World as I See It*, translated by Alan Harris (Secaucus, NJ), is perhaps the most famous. It was compiled in 1934 by Einstein's stepson-in-law Rudolf Kayser, who also wrote a semi-official biography of Einstein under the pseudonym Anton Reiser: *Albert Einstein: A Biographical Portrait* (London, 1931). Other Einstein collections include: *Out of My Later Years* (New York, 1950); *Ideas and Opinions*, translated by Sonja Bargmann (New York, 1954); and Otto Nathan and Heinz Norden (eds), *Einstein on Peace* (New York, 1960).

The sayings and aphorisms of Einstein are legion and, of course, many are apocryphal. At his best Einstein managed to be both profound and amusing, as in this from 1945–6: *I never worry about the future. It comes soon enough.* Two excellent collections are: Helen Dukas and Banesh Hoffmann (eds), *Albert Einstein, The Human Side: New Glimpses from his Archives* (Princeton, 1979); and Alice Calaprice (ed), *The Expanded Quotable Einstein* (Princeton, 2000). Editions of Einstein's correspondence include: *The Born-Einstein Letters*, translated by Irene Born (New York, 1971), and *Letters to Solovine, 1906–1955*, translated by Wade Baskin (New York, 1993). Jürgen Renn and Robert Schulmann's edition of *Albert Einstein / Mileva Marić: The Love Letters*, translated by Shawn Smith (Princeton, 1992), offers a revealing insight into the young Einstein and has an excellent introduction.

Two insightful accounts of Mileva's life are: Desanka Trbuhović-Gjurić, *Im Schatten Albert Einsteins: Das tragische Leben der Mileva Einstein-Maric* (Bern, 1983), and Michele Zackheim, *Einstein's Daughter: The Search for Lieserl* (New York, 1999). For a balanced summary of Mileva's scientific contribution to Einstein's work, see John Stachel, 'Albert Einstein and Mileva Marić: A Collaboration that Failed to Develop', *Creative Couples in the Sciences*, eds Helena M Pycior et al (New Brunswick, 1996), pp. 207–19.

The nearest Einstein came to writing his life story was in 1946 (a text he called his *obituary*), now available in a dual-language edition: Albert Einstein, *Autobiographical Notes: A Centennial Edition*, ed and trans Paul Arthur Schilpp (La Salle, 1979). A year before his death he wrote a brief postscript to this, which is published in Carl Seelig (ed), *Helle Zeit – Dunkle Zeit: In Memoriam Albert Einstein* (Zurich, 1956). Einstein's sister, Maja, wrote a delightful portrait of his early life and this is available in the *Collected Papers*: 'Albert Einstein: A Biographical Sketch', *CP* 1, trans, pp. xv–xxii.

Some of the most vivid and revealing biographies of Einstein were written by colleagues and friends. Of these the ones I have found most useful are: Philipp Frank, *Einstein: His Life and Times*, ed Shuichi Kusaka, trans George Rosen (New York, 1947); Peter Michelmore, *Einstein: Profile of the Man* (London, 1963); and Alexander Moszkowski, *Conversations with Einstein*, trans Henry L Brose (London, 1972); Carl Seelig, *Albert Einstein: A Documentary Biography*, trans Mervyn Savill (London, 1956); Antonina Vallentin, *Einstein: A Biography*, trans Moura Budberg (London, 1954).

Of the more recent biographies, Albrecht Fölsing's *Albert Einstein: A Biography*, trans Ewald Osers (Harmondsworth, 1998) is particularly good on Einstein's life in Europe, whereas Denis Brian's *Einstein: A Life* (New York, 1996) offers a detailed account of his experiences in America. Two books that reveal Einstein's private life are Friedrich Herneck's *Einstein Privat* (Berlin, 1978), and Roger Highfield and Paul Carter, *The Private Lives of Albert Einstein* (London, 1993). Dennis Overbye's *Einstein in Love: A Scientific Romance* (London, 2001) is a wonderfully written and perceptive account of both Einstein's life with Mileva and his early physics. Banesh Hoffmann's *Albert Einstein* (St Albans, 1977), written with Helen Dukas, is still a very readable introduction to both the science and the man. Rather more challenging is the late Abraham Pais's '*Subtle is the Lord . . .': The Science and the Life of Albert Einstein* (Oxford, 1982), an authoritative study that combines succinct biographical information with high-level physics. See also his *Einstein Lived Here* (Oxford, 1994) and *Niels Bohr's Times, in Physics, Philosophy, and Polity* (Oxford, 1991).

Einstein's *annus mirabilis*, 1905, was a unique year in the history of physics. An excellent translation of his papers together with illuminating commentaries is John Stachel et al (eds and trans), *Einstein's Miraculous Year: Five Papers that Changed the Face of Physics* (Princeton, 1998). L Pearce Williams has compiled a fine anthology contextualising Einstein's discoveries: *Relativity Theory: Its Origins and Impact on Modern Thought* (New York, 1968).

Lewis Pyenson's *The Young Einstein: The Advent of Relativity* (Bristol, 1985) provides invaluable background information about the Germany of Einstein's youth, and Fritz Stern's *Einstein's German World* (Harmondsworth, 2000) is equally useful on Weimar Germany. See also A P French (ed), *Einstein: A Centenary Volume* (London, 1979).

An excellent book that conveys the subtleties of both Einstein's mathematics and quantum theory is *It Must Be Beautiful: Great Equations of Modern Science*, ed Graham Farmelo (London, 2002). Harald Fritzsch uses an imaginary encounter between Newton and Einstein to explain the background to $E=mc^2$ in *An Equation that Changed the World: Newton, Einstein, and the Theory of Relativity*, trans Karin Huesch (Chicago, 1994). Also recommended are Joseph Schwartz and Michael McGuinness's cartoon-style *Introducing Einstein* (Icon, 1979) and Jeremy Bernstein's more conventional but equally accessible *Albert Einstein and the Frontiers of Physics* (Oxford, 1996). Physicist and novelist Alan Lightman offers a wide-ranging yet succinct introduction to the *Great Ideas in Physics* (New York, 1992) and his fiction work *Einstein's Dreams* (London, 1993) contains a series of thought experiments describing worlds in which time obeys different laws. On the subject of time, see Paul Davies's *About Time: Einstein's Unfinished Revolution* (Harmondsworth, 1995). For an introduction to the strange world of the quantum, see Manjit Kumar's article 'Quantum Reality', *Prometheus* 2 (1999), pp 52–64 and his forthcoming study of the subject *Quantum*. Richard Rhodes's Pulitzer prize-winning *The Making of the Atomic Bomb* (Harmondsworth, 1988) is the best account of the atomic bomb.

Einstein's influence extends far beyond science, as Gerald Holton shows in his article 'Einstein and the Shaping of our Imagination', in *Albert Einstein: Historical and Cultural Perspectives. The Centennial Symposium in Jerusalem*, eds Gerald Holton and Yehuda Elkana (Princeton, 1982), pp vii–xxxii. Alan J Friedman and Carol C Donley's *Einstein as Myth and Muse* (Cambridge, 1985) is still the best account of his influence on the arts. Einstein scholar Arthur I Miller's *Einstein, Picasso: Space, Time, and the Beauty That Causes Havoc* (New York, 2001) is a thought-provoking attempt to establish links between physics and modern art. I have explored literary responses to scientific ideas such as relativity and the new physics in 'Elective Affinity? A Tale of Two Cultures', *Prometheus* 4 (2001), pp 46–65, and *Metaphor and Materiality: German Literature and the World-View of Science 1780–1955* (Oxford, 2000).

The response of creative writers to Einstein's science is a fascinating subject in itself, and it is worth mentioning a couple of outstanding examples: Karel Čapek was one of the first to make use of relativity in novels such as *Krakatit* (1924) and *The Absolute at Large* (1927). Vladimir Nabokov's *Ada or Ardor* (London, 1969) is an evocative exploration of time, in which Einstein becomes 'Engelwein' and relativity 'the fiat of a fishy formula'. Historian of science Russell McCormmach's novel *Night Thoughts of a Classical Physicist* (Cambridge, Mass, 1982) captures the scientific Zeitgeist of Berlin in 1918. Nicholas Mosley's *Hopeful Monsters* (London, 1990) places the ideas of relativity and quantum theory into the very human context of lives torn apart by the chaotic course of European history. Anna McGrail's *Mrs Einstein* (London, 1998) imaginatively explores the Einstein myth from the perspective of the silent figure in his life: Lieserl. Finally, Nicolas Roeg's film *Insignificance* (1985) brings together Einstein and Marilyn Monroe in an encounter the great physicist would no doubt have enjoyed.

SELECTED WEBSITES

www.albert-einstein.org

The website of the Albert Einstein Archive, part of the Jewish National & University Library, at the Hebrew University of Jerusalem. Ze'ev Rosenkranz's book *Albert Through the Looking-Glass: The Personal Papers of Albert Einstein* (Jerusalem, 1998) offers a fascinating glimpse of the materials in the Archive, with many photographs and facsimiles of documents. This excellent website has biographical information, bibliographical resources and even a kids' page.

http://stripe.colorado.edu/~judy/einstein.html

A website of Einstein quotations including this anonymous limerick:

> There's a wonderful family named Stein,
> There's Ep, there's Gert, and there's Ein.
> Ep's statues are junk,
> Gert's poems are bunk,
> And nobody understands Ein.

http://www.livingreviews.org
This is the website for *Living Reviews in Relativity*, an online journal on the science of relativity produced by The Max Planck Institute for Gravitational Physics (Albert Einstein Institute), Potsdam (**www.aei-potsdam.mpg.de/about/index.html**). The serious student of Einstein can search and access articles on many aspects of the science.

www.pbs.org/wgbh/nova/einstein
Website for the NOVA program *Einstein Revealed*, originally broadcast in October 1996. Includes games, articles, and teachers' notes.

www.princetonhistory.org/einstein/index.html
Details of Einstein's life in Princeton.

http://foia.fbi.gov/einstein.htm
From this page you can view and download Einstein's FBI files. Well worth a visit.

www.aip.org/history/einstein
Good biographical site with many photographs set up by the American Institute of Physics.

www-gap.dcs.st-and.ac.uk/~history/Mathematicians/Einstein.html
School of Mathematics and Statistics at the University of St Andrews, Scotland. Explains the mathematical context to the science with pages on many key figures in the story of relativity.

www.th.physik.uni-frankfurt.de/~jr/physpiceinstein.html
Website of black and white photographs of Einstein.

Acknowledgements

I am particularly grateful to Manjit Kumar for reading parts of the manuscript as well as for many enjoyable discussions about physics and physicists. Many thanks to Ian Pindar for his expert editing, and to Stephen Brown and Barbara Schwepcke at Haus Publishing. I am also grateful to Graham Nelson and Paul Bishop, as well as to Barbara Wolff at the Albert Einstein Archives and to Diana K Buchwald at the Einstein Papers Project. Finally, thanks also to Susan, whose help and support was as ever invaluable

Picture Sources

The author and publishers wish to express their thanks to the following sources of illustrative material and/or permission to reproduce it. They will make proper acknowledgements in future editions in the event that any omissions have occurred.

Topham Picturepoint: pp. iii, vi, 3, 5, 11, 18, 20, 24, 35, 56, 67, 74, 77, 96, 106, 117, 125; Corbis-Bettman-UPI: pp. 32, 83, 116, 130; Ann Ronan Picture Library: pp. 40, 57, 62, 68, 98; Hulton Archive: p. 56

Index